my World Social Studies TEXAS

We Explore People and Places

PEARSON

Boston, Massachusetts
Chandler, Arizona
Glenview, Illinois
New York, New York

It's my story, too!

You are one of the authors of this book. You can write in this book! You can take notes in this book! You can draw in it, too! This book will be yours to keep.

Print your name, school, and city or town below. Then write to tell everyone all about you.

Name

School

City or Town

All About Me

Credits appear on pages **R33–R34,** which constitute an extension of this copyright page.

Copyright © 2016 Pearson Education, Inc., or its affiliates. All Rights Reserved. Printed in the United States of America. This publication is protected by copyright, and permission should be obtained from the publisher prior to any prohibited reproduction, storage in a retrieval system, or transmission in any form or by any means, electronic, mechanical, photocopying, recording, or otherwise. For information regarding permissions, request forms, and the appropriate contacts within the Pearson Education Global Rights & Permissions department, please visit www.pearsoned.com/permissions/.

PEARSON, ALWAYS LEARNING, and myWORLD SOCIAL STUDIES are exclusive trademarks owned by Pearson Education, Inc. or its affiliates in the U.S. and/or other countries.

Softcover: ISBN-13: 978-0-328-81458-9
ISBN-10: 0-328-81458-X
13 18

Hardcover: ISBN-13: 978-0-328-84905-5
ISBN-10: 0-328-84905-7
1 2 3 4 5 6 7 8 9 10 V011 19 18 17 16 15

Pearson *Texas myWorld Social Studies* was developed especially for Texas with the help of teachers from across the state and covers 100 percent of the Texas Essential Knowledge and Skills for Social Studies. This story began with a series of teacher roundtables in cities across the state of Texas that inspired a program blueprint for *Texas myWorld Social Studies*. In addition, Judy Brodigan served as our expert advisor, guiding our creation of a dynamic Social Studies curriculum for TEKS mastery. Once this blueprint was finalized, a dedicated team—made up of Pearson authors, content experts, and social studies teachers from Texas—worked to bring our collective vision into reality.

Pearson would like to extend a special thank you to all of the teachers who helped guide the development of this program. We gratefully acknowledge your efforts to realize the possibilities of elementary Social Studies teaching and learning. Together, we will prepare Texas students for their future roles in college, careers, and as active citizens.

Program Consulting Authors

The Colonial Williamsburg Foundation
Williamsburg VA

Armando Cantú Alonzo
Associate Professor of History
Texas A&M University
College Station TX

Dr. Linda Bennett
Associate Professor, Department of Learning, Teaching, & Curriculum
College of Education
University of Missouri
Columbia MO

Dr. James B. Kracht
Byrne Chair for Student Success
Executive Associate Dean
College of Education and Human Development
College of Education
Texas A&M University
College Station TX

Dr. William E. White
Vice President for Productions, Publications and Learning Ventures
The Colonial Williamsburg Foundation
Williamsburg VA

Reviewers and Consultants

ACADEMIC REVIEWERS

Kathy Glass
Author, *Lesson Design for Differentiated Instruction*
President, Glass Educational Consulting
Woodside CA

Roberta Logan
African Studies Specialist
Retired, Boston Public Schools/ Mission Hill School
Boston MA

Jeanette Menendez
Reading Coach
Doral Academy Elementary
Miami FL

Bob Sandman
Adjunct Assistant Professor of Business and Economics
Wilmington College—Cincinnati Branches
Blue Ash OH

PROGRAM CONSULTANT

Judy Brodigan
Former President, Texas Council for Social Studies
Grapevine TX

Padre Island National Seashore

CONNECT

Master the TEKS with a personal connection.

myStory Spark

The **myStory Book** writing strand in the program begins with a **myStory Spark** activity. Here you can record your initial ideas about the **Big Question**.

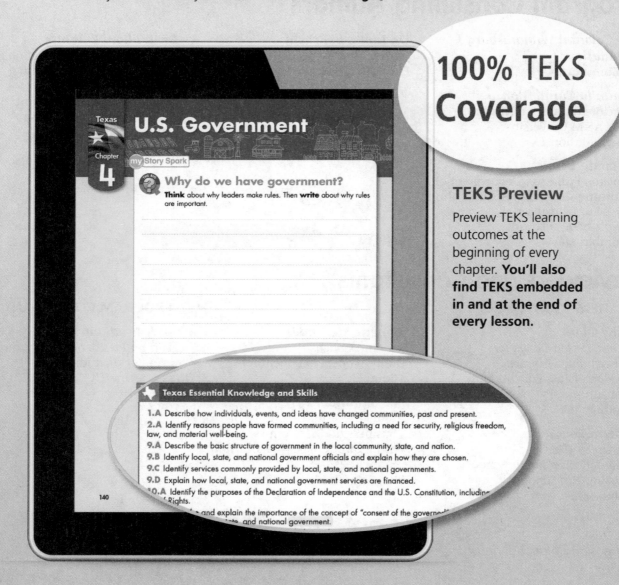

100% TEKS Coverage

Texas ★ Chapter 4

U.S. Government

myStory Spark

Why do we have government?
Think about why leaders make rules. Then **write** about why rules are important.

140

Texas Essential Knowledge and Skills

1.A Describe how individuals, events, and ideas have changed communities, past and present.
2.A Identify reasons people have formed communities, including a need for security, religious freedom, law, and material well-being.
9.A Describe the basic structure of government in the local community, state, and nation.
9.B Identify local, state, and national government officials and explain how they are chosen.
9.C Identify services commonly provided by local, state, and national governments.
9.D Explain how local, state, and national government services are financed.
10.A Identify the purposes of the Declaration of Independence and the U.S. Constitution, including ... Rights.
... and explain the importance of the concept of "consent of the governed" ... and national government.

TEKS Preview

Preview TEKS learning outcomes at the beginning of every chapter. **You'll also find TEKS embedded in and at the end of every lesson.**

Lesson List

Lesson 1 America's First Peoples
Lesson 2 Early Explorers
Lesson 3 Early Spanish Communities
Lesson 4 Early French Communities
Lesson 5 Early English Communities
Lesson 6 Creating a New Nation

Mission San Luis
A Multicultural Community

From about 1560 to 1690, there were more than 100 Spanish missions built throughout Florida. A mission is a settlement that has a church where religion is taught. One of the most famous missions is Mission San Luis. Located in Tallahassee, it is one of the last remaining mission sites today. "It's also the only place where both the Apalachee and the Spaniards lived together," says Grace. The Apalachee are Native Americans and Spaniards are people from Spain. "I love learning about other cultures," she adds. No one lives at the mission anymore, but it has been rebuilt. Visitors can tour the mission and watch people act out what life was like there hundreds of years ago.

"Native Americans and Spaniards shared this mission," Grace explains. At that time, Native Americans and European settlers usually did not live together. Mission San Luis was special.

Grace was excited to visit one of the last remaining missions.

myStory Video

Move seamlessly from **the Student Worktext** to technology! Watch the myStory Videos to explore the **Big Question** and key ideas in the chapter.

Access the TEKS

Texas *myWorld Social Studies* covers the TEKS in all formats. Access the content through the printed worktext, eText, or online with the digital course on Realize.

PEARSON realize Go online at: www.PearsonTexas.com

Every lesson is supported by digital activities, myStory Videos, vocabulary activities, and myStory Book on Tikatok.

EXPERIENCE

Enjoy social studies while practicing the TEKS.

Student Interactive Worktext

With the Texas *myWorld Social Studies* worktext, you'll love writing, drawing, circling and underlining in your own book.

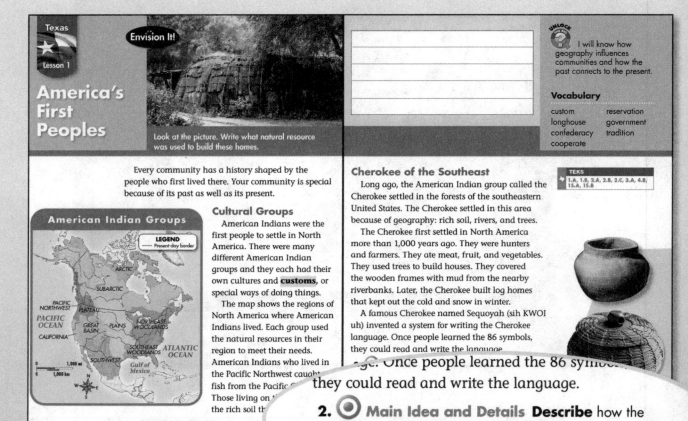

Texas
Lesson 1

Envision It!

America's First Peoples

Look at the picture. Write what natural resource was used to build these homes.

Every community has a history shaped by the people who first lived there. Your community is special because of its past as well as its present.

American Indian Groups

LEGEND
Present-day border

ARCTIC
SUBARCTIC
PACIFIC NORTHWEST
PLATEAU
PACIFIC OCEAN
GREAT BASIN
PLAINS
NORTHEAST WOODLANDS
CALIFORNIA
SOUTHWEST
SOUTHEAST WOODLANDS
ATLANTIC OCEAN
Gulf of Mexico

1,000 mi
1,000 km

Cultural Groups

American Indians were the first people to settle in North America. There were many different American Indian groups and they each had their own cultures and **customs**, or special ways of doing things.

The map shows the regions of North America where American Indians lived. Each group used the natural resources in their region to meet their needs. American Indians who lived in the Pacific Northwest caught fish from the Pacific Those living on the rich soil th

1. Identify and underline two ways A used natural resources to live.

UNLOCK
I will know how geography influences communities and how the past connects to the present.

Vocabulary

custom   reservation
longhouse   government
confederacy   tradition
cooperate

Cherokee of the Southeast

Long ago, the American Indian group called the Cherokee settled in the forests of the southeastern United States. The Cherokee settled in this area because of geography: rich soil, rivers, and trees.

The Cherokee first settled in North America more than 1,000 years ago. They were hunters and farmers. They ate meat, fruit, and vegetables. They used trees to build houses. They covered the wooden frames with mud from the nearby riverbanks. Later, the Cherokee built log homes that kept out the cold and snow in winter.

A famous Cherokee named Sequoyah (sih KWOI uh) invented a system for writing the Cherokee language. Once people learned the 86 symbols, they could read and write the language.

TEKS
1.A, 1.B, 2.A, 2.B, 2.C, 3.A, 4.B, 15.A, 15.B

...ge. Once people learned the 86 symbols, they could read and write the language.

2. **Main Idea and Details** **Describe** how the Cherokee created a new community.

Target Reading Skills

The worktext enables you to practice important **Target Reading Skills**—essential skills you'll need when reading informational texts. Reinforce your ELA TEKS during the social studies block of time.

PEARSON realize **Go online at:**
www.PearsonTexas.com

Every lesson is supported by digital activities, myStory Videos, vocabulary activities, and myStory Book on Tikatok.

Leveled Readers

Engaging leveled readers are available in print and digital formats on Realize.

Digital Activities

Every lesson includes a **Digital Activity** that helps support the Big Idea.

UNDERSTAND

Assess TEKS and demonstrate understanding.

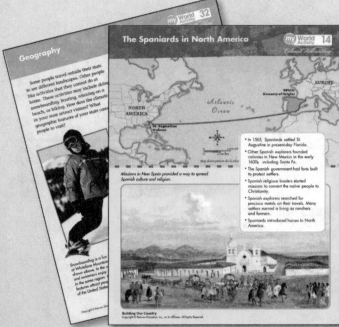

myWorld Activities

Work together in small groups on activities that range from mapping, graphing, and role playing, to read-alouds and analyzing primary sources. Digital versions of innovative hands-on activities for each chapter can be found on Realize.

Find **TEKS practice** at the end of every chapter.

myStory Book

The **myStory Book** final writing activity gives you the exciting opportunity to write and illustrate your own digital book. Go to **www.Tikatok.com/ myWorldSocialStudies** to learn more.

Every lesson is supported by digital activities, myStory Videos, vocabulary activities, and myStory Book on Tikatok.

Go online at:
www.PearsonTexas.com

Celebrating Texas and the Nation is also supported by the interactive eText.

My Community, My Country

PEARSON realize Go online at:
www.PearsonTexas.com

- ▶ **Interactive eText**
- ▶ **Big Question Activity**
  How do people best cooperate?
- ▶ **myStory Video**
  How do people best cooperate?
- ▶ **Song**
  Lyrics and Music
- ▶ **Vocabulary Preview**
- ▶ **Lesson Introduction**
- ▶ **Digital Got it? Activity**
- ▶ **Digital Skill Lessons**
  Draw Conclusions
  Taking Action
- ▶ **Vocabulary Review**
- ▶ **myStory Book on Tikatok**
  www.tikatok.com/
  myWorldSocialStudies
- ▶ **Chapter Tests**

BALLOT BOX

? **How do people best cooperate?**

Texas

Chapter

2

Working to Meet Our Needs

PEARSON realize Go online at:
www.PearsonTexas.com

- ▶ Interactive eText
- ▶ **Big Question Activity**
  How do people get what they need?
- ▶ **myStory Video**
  How do people get what they need?
- ▶ **Song**
  Lyrics and Music
- ▶ Vocabulary Preview
- ▶ Lesson Introduction
- ▶ Digital Got it? Activity
- ▶ **Digital Skill Lessons**
  Main Idea and Details
  Reading a Flowchart
- ▶ Vocabulary Review
- ▶ **myStory Book on Tikatok**
  www.tikatok.com/
  myWorldSocialStudies
- ▶ Chapter Tests

? How do people get what they need?

The World Around Us

PEARSON realize Go online at:
www.PearsonTexas.com

- ▶ Interactive eText
- ▶ Big Question Activity
  What is the world like?
- ▶ myStory Video
  What is the world like?
- ▶ Song
  Lyrics and Music
- ▶ Vocabulary Preview
- ▶ Lesson Introduction
- ▶ Digital Got it? Activity
- ▶ Digital Skill Lessons
  Cause and Effect
  Using a Map Scale
- ▶ Vocabulary Review
- ▶ myStory Book on Tikatok
  www.tikatok.com/
  myWorldSocialStudies
- ▶ Chapter Tests

Texas

Chapter 4

Celebrating Our Traditions

? How is culture shared?

Our Nation Past and Present

PEARSON realize Go online at:
www.PearsonTexas.com

- ▷ **Interactive eText**
- ▷ **Big Question Activity**
  How does life change throughout history?
- ▷ **myStory Video**
  How does life change throughout history?
- ▷ **Song**
  Lyrics and Music
- ▷ **Vocabulary Preview**
- ▷ **Lesson Introduction**
- ▷ **Digital Got it? Activity**
- ▷ **Digital Skill Lessons**
  Fact and Opinion
  Reading a Timeline
- ▷ **Vocabulary Review**
- ▷ **myStory Book on Tikatok**
  www.tikatok.com/
  myWorldSocialStudies
- ▷ **Chapter Tests**

Keys to Good Writing

The Writing Process

Good writers follow steps when they write. Here are five steps that will help you become a good writer!

Prewrite	Plan your writing.
Draft	Write your first draft.
Revise	Make your writing better.
Edit	Check your writing.
Share	Share your writing with others.

21st Century Learning Checklist

21C

You can go online to www.PearsonTexas.com to practice the skills listed below. These are skills that will be important to you throughout your life. After you complete each skill tutorial online, check it off here in your Worktext.

◉ Target Reading Skills

- ☐ Main Idea and Details
- ☐ Cause and Effect
- ☐ Classify and Categorize
- ☐ Fact and Opinion
- ☐ Draw Conclusions
- ☐ Generalize
- ☐ Compare and Contrast
- ☐ Sequence
- ☐ Summarize

Collaboration and Creativity Skills

- ☐ Solve Problems
- ☐ Work in Cooperative Teams
- ☐ Resolve Conflict
- ☐ Generate New Ideas

Graph Skills

- ☐ Interpret Graphs
- ☐ Create Charts
- ☐ Interpret Timelines

Map Skills

- ☐ Use Longitude and Latitude
- ☐ Interpret Physical Maps
- ☐ Interpret Economic Data on Maps
- ☐ Interpret Cultural Data on Maps

Critical Thinking Skills

- ☐ Compare Viewpoints
- ☐ Use Primary and Secondary Sources
- ☐ Identify Bias
- ☐ Make Decisions
- ☐ Predict Consequences

Media and Technology Skills

- ☐ Conduct Research
- ☐ Use the Internet Safely
- ☐ Analyze Images
- ☐ Evaluate Media Content
- ☐ Deliver an Effective Presentation

Celebrate Freedom
Bill of Rights

TEKS 19.A, 19.B

Vocabulary

amendment

The United States Constitution has 27 **amendments,** or parts that were added to the Constitution after it was first written. The first ten amendments are called the Bill of Rights. The Bill of Rights lists rights that citizens have.

One right says that we can say and write what we think. This is called "freedom of speech." We can also get together in groups. We have the right to ask the government to change things we do not like. We can choose our own religion, too. The Bill of Rights also says that we have a right to be safe in our homes.

1

My Favorite Right

1. Work with a partner. Choose one of the rights you have learned about.

2. Draw a picture of the right or make a slideshow.

3. Write a sentence or two explaining what the right is and why it is important.

4. Share your picture or slideshow with the class. Keep these tips in mind.

   - Speak loudly.

   - Speak clearly.

   - Look at the audience.

   - Listen to others.

BILL OF RIGHTS

Right to say what you want

The Arts in Texas
Stories and Poems

TEKS 15.A, 15.B, 19.B

Vocabulary

heritage

Buck Ramsey was a cowboy in Texas. Two of his poems are *Anthem* and *Christmas Waltz*. They tell what it was like to be a cowboy in Texas.

Anthem by Buck Ramsey

I lived in time with horse hoof falling;
I listened well and heard the calling
The earth, my mother, bade to me,
Though I would still ride wild and free.

1. **Identify** two of Ramsey's poems. **Explain** the significance of the selected poems of the local cultural heritage.

2. **Write** a poem and **draw** a picture to go with it.

Visual Art

Theodore Gentilz was a French painter. In 1844, he was hired to help start a new colony in Texas.

He brought his paints and brushes with him, and he painted scenes all over Texas, and even Mexico! He painted pictures of American Indians, Mexican ranchers, and Spanish churches. His paintings show the culture and **heritage,** or traditions, of Texas.

3. With a partner, do an Internet keyword search to identify the paintings *Empanadas* and *Barbacoa para cumpleaños* by the Texas artist Carmen Lomas Garza. **Explain** how these paintings show the artist's Texas heritage, and explain the significance of the selected paintings of the local cultural heritage.

Sculptures

Elisabet Ney was born in Germany. Her father was a stonecutter. He taught her about being an artist. Ney learned how to make sculptures out of stone.

Ney came to the United States in 1870. She opened an art studio in Austin, Texas. She was asked to make statues of Sam Houston and Stephen Austin, two very important men in Texas's history. Her studio has been turned into a museum that anyone can visit.

4. On a separate piece of paper identify two statues by Elisabet Ney. Explain the significance, or importance, of the statues you selected.

Symbols of Texas

The flag of Texas is a **patriotic** symbol. It shows love and support for our state.

The mockingbird is the state bird of Texas. One kind of mockingbird can sing as many as 200 songs.

The bluebonnet is the state flower of Texas. You can find bluebonnets across Texas.

5. Circle the names of the Texas state bird and state flower.

6. On a separate sheet of paper, **compare and contrast** the Texas flag and the United States flag.

Vocabulary

patriotic

6

Another symbol of Texas is the Pledge to the Texas Flag. When we say the words to the pledge, we are being patriotic.

Honor the Texas flag;
I pledge allegiance to thee,
Texas, one state under God,
one and indivisible.

Texas also has a state tree. A former Texas governor wanted a pecan tree to be planted in his memory. He wanted nuts from that tree to be planted to make Texas "a land of trees." The pecan tree was made the state tree in 1919.

7. Recite the Pledge to the Texas Flag.

Landmarks and Monuments

🔶 TEKS 1.B

Vocabulary

landmark

monument

Landmarks mark an important place.
Monuments honor important people,
events, or ideas.

The Alamo was used as a fort
during Texas's fight for
independence from Mexico.
The Alamo still exists today as
a memorial for the heroes of
the revolution.

The Alamo

The Tejano Monument at the Texas Capitol
in Austin honors the role of Tejanos in the
history of Texas. A *Tejano* is a Texan of
Mexican origin.

The Tejano Monument

8. Choose your favorite
   monument or landmark.
   On a separate sheet of
   paper, **explain** why
   it is important.

The Texas State Capitol in downtown Austin is the building where our state government meets and works. It is also an important Texas landmark. It is the largest state capitol in the United States. When it was built, it was the seventh largest building in the world!

The World War II Memorial is in Washington, D.C. It honors men and women who fought and died for our country's freedom in World War II. The memorial has pillars, or columns, for each state.

9. **Explain** why the Texas State Capitol is important.

_____

_____

_____

_____

Celebrating Texas and the Nation

Texas on Maps and Globes

TEKS 6.B

Maps show information about an area. They can show the **coast,** or the place where land and water meet.

Look at the map title at the top of the map. It tells you what the map shows. You can use the legend to help you find places on the map.

Vocabulary

map
coast
globe

10. **Draw** an X to show where you live.

11. **Circle** the capital of Texas.

12. **Underline** the names of four other cities.

13. **Trace** the coast of Texas with a pencil.

Texas, Political

10

A **globe** is a model of Earth. A model is a small copy of something. Just like our planet, a globe is round. Like maps, globes show water, land, countries, states, and cities. You may have a globe in your classroom.

Look at the picture of a globe. It shows one half of Earth. Now look at Texas on the globe. Like maps, many globes have a legend. You can use the legend to help you find cities and the capital.

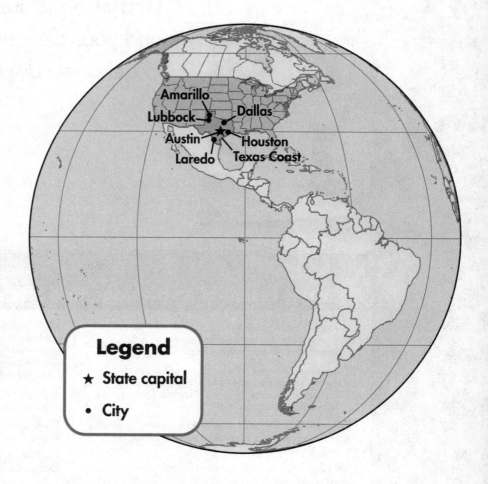

Legend
★ State capital
• City

14. **Find** a globe in your school, library, or home. Use it to locate the following five places: Texas, your community, Houston, the capital of Texas, and the coast of Texas.

My Community, My Country

THE BIG ?

How do people best cooperate?

Draw a picture of how you and your classmates cooperate to get a job done.

Texas Essential Knowledge and Skills

1.B Identify and explain the significance of various community, state, and national landmarks such as monuments and government buildings.

6.B Locate places of significance, including the local community, Texas, the state capital, the U.S. capital, major cities in Texas, the coast of Texas, Canada, Mexico, and the United States on maps and globes.

11.A Identify functions of governments such as establishing order, providing security, and managing conflict.

11.B Identify governmental services in the community such as police and fire protection, libraries, schools, and parks and explain their value to the community.

11.C Describe how governments tax citizens to pay for services.

12.A Name current public officials, including mayor, governor, and president.

12.B Compare the roles of public officials, including mayor, governor, and president.

12.C Identify ways that public officials are selected, including election and appointment to office.

12.D Identify how citizens participate in their own governance through staying informed of what public officials are doing, providing input to them, and volunteering to participate in government functions.

13.A Identify characteristics of good citizenship, including truthfulness, justice, equality, respect for oneself and others, responsibility in daily life, and participation in government by educating oneself about the issues, respectfully holding public officials to their word, and voting.

13.D Identify ways to actively practice good citizenship, including involvement in community service.

14.A Recite the Pledge of Allegiance to the United States Flag and the Pledge to the Texas Flag.

14.B Identify selected patriotic songs, including "The Star Spangled Banner" and "America the Beautiful."

14.C Identify selected symbols such as state and national birds and flowers and patriotic symbols such as the U.S. and Texas flags and Uncle Sam.

14.D Identify how selected customs, symbols, and celebrations reflect an American love of individualism, inventiveness, and freedom.

18.A Obtain information about a topic using a variety of valid oral sources such as conversations, interviews, and music.

18.E Interpret oral, visual, and print material by identifying the main idea, predicting, and comparing and contrasting.

20.A Use a problem-solving process to identify a problem, gather information, list and consider options, consider advantages and disadvantages, choose and implement a solution, and evaluate the effectiveness of the solution.

 # Begin With a Song

Our Country Today

Sing to the tune of "Rockabye, Baby."

When people vote
They each make a choice.
We are all citizens.
We have a voice.

We elect people
To serve and to lead.
With honesty and fairness
In action and deed.

Vote Here

PEARSON
realize   Go online to access your interactive digital lesson.

13

Vocabulary Preview

citizen

respect

responsible

government

rights

Identify examples of these words and **circle** them in the picture.

PRESIDENT'S HALL

VALLEY FORGE

GIFT SHOP

Congress

SUPREME COURT

ELEVATOR

law

court

Congress

symbol

independence

15

We Are Good Citizens

Envision It!

Circle examples of people who are taking care of the things around them.

TEKS
13.A, 13.D

A **community** is a place where people work, live, or play together. Your school is one kind of community. A **citizen** is a member of a community, state, and country.

Ways to Be a Good Citizen

Good citizens care about themselves and others. They listen to one another. They also help one another. A good citizen shows **respect,** or concern for others. When you are fair, or just, and honest with others, you are being a good citizen.

1. **Describe** good citizens.

Good citizens are _____

_____

We respect others when we share.

UNLOCK THE BIG ?

I will know ways to be a good citizen.

Vocabulary

community
citizen
respect
responsible

Good Citizens at School

There are many ways to be a good citizen at school. You can listen to other people's ideas. This shows that you have respect for them. You can share your own ideas. You can also help clean up and take care of school supplies.

You can be a good citizen on the playground, too. Be sure to take turns and be fair when playing. Remember to follow the rules and tell the truth. Rules tell us what to do and what not to do.

2. ◉ **Main Idea and Details**
Underline two ways you can be a good citizen in school.

Good citizens are fair and take turns.

Citizens in the Community

You are a citizen of your community. Communities can be different sizes. A town is a small community. A city is a big community.

There are many ways you and your family can help in your community. You can help plant trees in a park. You can help clean up a playground.

The people who live near you are part of your neighborhood. They are called neighbors. You can help make your neighborhood a nice place to live. You can pick up trash. You can help a neighbor rake leaves. You can say hello and talk to people you know.

A mural, or painted wall, can make a community more beautiful.

It is important to be a responsible citizen. **Responsible** means taking care of important things. When you clean your room, you are being responsible at home. When you help clean up a park, you are being responsible in your community.

3. **Draw** a picture of how you can help in your community.

Got it?

TEKS 13.A

4. ● **Draw Conclusions** Why is it important to be a good citizen?

_____

- -

_____

5. ? **Write** something you and your classmates can do to be responsible citizens.

my Story Ideas

_____

- -

_____

_____

_____

6. **Identify** what makes a good citizen.

_____

- -

_____

Taking Action

Good citizens help solve problems in their communities. They find out what the problems are. Then they take action to solve the problem.

The children below have a problem. Their school does not have bike racks. Here are the steps they took to help solve their problem.

1. Children ride their bikes to school. There is no place to keep the bikes there.

2. Children discuss options with the principal. They decide that a bake sale can help raise money.

3. Children raise enough money at the bake sale to buy bike racks.

4. Now the children can keep their bikes at school. Their solution worked.

TEKS

SS 20.A Use a problem-solving process to identify a problem, gather information, and choose and implement a solution.

ELA 15.B Use common graphic features to assist in the interpretation of text.

Try it!

1. **Look** at the pictures. **Write** how the children solved their problem.

_____

_____

_____

2. **Draw** a picture of citizens in your community taking action to solve a problem.

PEARSON realize Go online to access your interactive digital lesson.

21

Our Rights as Citizens

Look at the pictures.

TEKS
11.A, 12.D, 13.A, 13.D, 18.E

Our country is called the United States of America. People who are born here are citizens of the United States. People who are not born here can apply to become citizens and take an oath of allegiance.

Our Government

A long time ago, our country's leaders wrote a plan for our country. This plan is called the United States Constitution. The Constitution tells us how to run our government. A **government** is a group of people who work together to run a city, a state, or a country. The Constitution tells us how to make laws that keep us safe and help us get along.

These people are becoming citizens of the United States of America.

1. ⊙ **Main Idea** <u>Underline</u> two reasons the Constitution is important to United States citizens.

UNLOCK
THE BIG
?

I will know the rights that American citizens have.

Vocabulary

government · · · · · · · · · vote
rights · · · · · · · · · · · · freedom

Tell what is happening in each picture.

Our Basic Rights

All citizens in the United States have equal, or the same, rights. **Rights** are things we are free to do. The government cannot take away rights.

Since citizens have equal rights, they should be treated the same way. The rules and laws in our country are the same for everyone. This is called equality.

Citizens have the right to vote. To **vote** means to make a choice about something. In the United States, citizens choose their leaders by voting.

Citizens vote to choose their leaders.

2. Write one right of citizens in our country.

_____

_____

_____

_____

PEARSON
realize™   Go online to access your
interactive digital lesson.

23

The Bill of Rights

The Constitution does more than tell us how to run our government. It also tells us the rights shared by all United States citizens. Ten of these rights are listed in a part of the Constitution called the Bill of Rights. The Bill of Rights protects our freedom. **Freedom** is the right to choose what we do and say.

The Bill of Rights says that citizens in the United States are free to say and write what we want as long as it does not harm others. It also says that we can choose our own religion. We are free to meet other people in public places. We are free to speak up when we disagree with our government. We can ask our government to fix things we think are wrong.

3. **Identify** and circle the rights you see in this picture.

Participating in Government

There are many ways that citizens can participate, or take part, in government. Voting is one way. You must be 18 years old to vote. You must also be a United States citizen.

There are other ways to participate in government. You can read and learn about the issues that are important. One issue could be whether to buy more books and computers for your school. Another could be how to make the water you drink safer.

You can read about or listen to what public officials are doing about the issues. You can let public officials know what you think about issues. You can give your input, or your opinion.

4. **Write** about an issue in your community or school that is important to you.

_____

_____

_____

_____

_____

You might think it is important to clean up a community park. What can you do to take part? You can write to public officials in your community. You can tell them about the park.

You can volunteer to help clean up the park. When you volunteer, you help out and do not get paid for the work you do. When you do volunteer work to help your community, it is called community service.

If public officials agree to help get the park cleaned up, you can make sure that happens. You can check to see that they stand by their word, or do what they promised to do. It is important to do so respectfully, or politely.

5. Write ways citizens can take part in government.

TEKS 13.A, 18.E

6. Main Idea and Details What is the Bill of Rights?

7. Which right is the most important to you? **List** one reason for your choice.

my Story Ideas

8. What is equality?

PEARSON
realize
Go online to access your
interactive digital lesson.
27

We Follow Rules and Laws

Look at the pictures.

TEKS
11.A

Think about a classroom where everyone is talking at the same time. Children are running around. No one takes turns or shares. This would not be a good place to learn.

School Rules

Your school has rules that help make it a good place for you to learn. Rules remind us how to be good school citizens. Rules also keep us safe. One rule tells us to take turns when talking. Another rule tells us not to run in the hall. You show respect for others and yourself when you follow rules.

1. **Write** one rule you follow at school.

_____

_____

_____

_____

Write what these pictures tell you about some rules in a community.

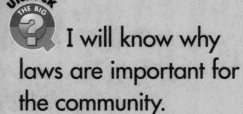
Vocabulary

law

court

consequence

Community Laws

Rules in a community are called laws. A **law** is a rule that everyone must follow. Leaders in our communities help make the laws. Creating laws is one function of government.

Laws help keep us safe and secure. They keep order. They help to stop conflicts, or problems. It is the law that cars and bikes have to stop at a stop sign. Wearing a seat belt is an important law in many places in the United States.

Laws remind people to be responsible. In many places, the law says people may not throw trash on the street. This law helps keep the community clean.

Most states have laws that say we must wear seat belts.

2. ◉ **Main Idea and Details**
   <u>Underline</u> two laws that keep us safe.

Why Laws Are Important

Laws are important because they protect our rights and keep us safe from harm. When the laws are not followed, people can get hurt.

In many places, it is a law to wear a helmet when you ride a bike. Following that law helps keep you safe. Drivers of cars must follow laws, too. They must stop at crosswalks and stop signs.

When people do not follow laws they might have to go to a court. A **court** is one part of our government. People who work in courts decide if someone has broken, or not followed, the law.

3. **Draw** an X on laws you see in this picture.

A **consequence** is something that happens as a result of an action. A person who breaks the law can have rights taken away. They might be required to pay a fine, or money, to the community. These consequences remind us that good citizens are responsible for their actions and respect the rights of others.

NO LITTERING VIOLATORS WILL BE PROSECUTED

4.  **Cause and Effect** <u>Underline</u> one thing that can happen when people do not follow laws.

Got it?

⬤ TEKS 11.A

5. ◉ **Draw Conclusions** Why is it important to have laws?

_____

_____

_____

_____

6. ❓ **Write** two laws in your community.

my Story Ideas

_____

_____

_____

_____

7. **Identify** and write one function of government.

_____

_____

Draw Conclusions

Details give us information about something.

To draw a conclusion, we think about details or facts and come to a decision about what the details and facts mean.

Detail: The children make snow angels.

Detail: The children help shovel snow off the sidewalk.

Conclusion: The children like to be outside in the snow.

Detail: The children build a snowman.

TEKS

SS 18.E Interpret visual and print material by identifying the main idea and predicting.
ELA 13 Students analyze and draw conclusions about the author's purpose and provide evidence from the text.

Look at the pictures below and **read** the details.
Write a conclusion about laws on the lines below.

Detail: It is a law to wear a seat belt in a car.

Detail: People must wear helmets when they ride bikes.

Detail: It is a law that drivers must stop at stop signs.

Conclusion:

_____

_____

_____

_____

_____

_____

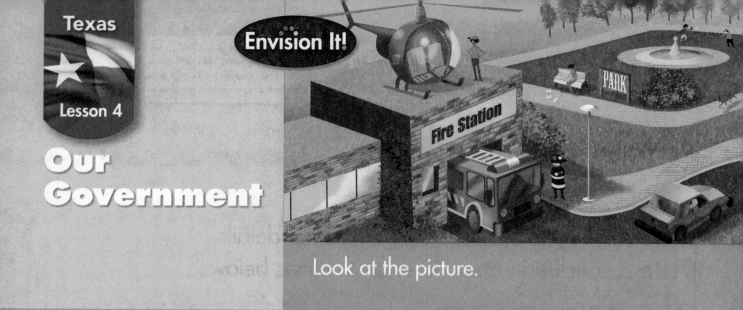

Our Government

Envision It!

Look at the picture.

TEKS
1.B, 11.A, 11.B, 11.C, 12.C

Parks are valuable to the community.

A government is a group of people who work together to run a community, state, or country. The Constitution tells us that citizens of the United States are responsible for their government. Citizens vote to elect leaders who will make good decisions that keep us safe and protect our rights.

Community Government

A community government works for a city or town. It keeps the city running smoothly and makes sure that citizens get services. A **service** is something that is done for you. Schools, libraries, parks, and fire stations are important and valuable to the community because they provide services. Citizens pay **taxes,** or money, to the government to pay for these services.

1. **Underline** two things governments do.

Put a ☑ on the places you have in your community.

UNLOCK THE BIG ?

I will know how the government gives communities what they need.

Vocabulary

service   Congress
tax   Supreme Court

State Government

A state government makes decisions that affect all the communities in one state. Different communities have different needs. A small town might need only one school, but a big city would need many.

The government of each state is located in its capital. State leaders make laws and decide which services to provide for its citizens. A police force is one government service all cities and states have. The police protect the people in the state.

2. ● **Main Idea and Details Identify** and **underline** two services that are provided by state governments.

This is the Texas State Capitol in Austin, Texas.

Congress meets
to vote on laws.

United States Government

Our government has three parts, called branches. Each branch has a different job. The president is the head of one branch of our country's government. The president leads the country and signs new laws.

Another branch of government is Congress. **Congress** is made up of leaders who write and vote on new laws. Citizens in each state vote for their members of Congress. Members of Congress work in the Capitol, a building in Washington, D.C.

Courts are another branch of government. The **Supreme Court** is the highest court in our country. Nine Supreme Court judges decide if the laws are fair. They also make sure that laws agree with the Constitution.

3. Write the job for each branch of government.

Branches of Government	
President	
Congress	
Supreme Court	

36

Landmarks

The people who work in our country's government are important. Government buildings are, too. A landmark is a structure that is important to a particular place. One example of a landmark is the United States Capitol. In Texas, there is a capitol, too. Every state in our country has one. In this building, government leaders meet and work.

Other national landmarks include the White House. This is the building where the president lives. Even a special ship can be a landmark. The USS *Elissa* is a national landmark. It is in Galveston, Texas. Many people came to our country through the port of Galveston. The ship honors this special place in our country.

USS *Elissa*

The White House

Monuments

Another kind of structure honors someone or something important to our country. A monument honors a person or event. The Washington Monument is in Washington, D.C. It honors our first president, George Washington.

The Statue of Liberty is another national monument. It stands in New York Harbor. The statue honors our country's freedom. France gave the statue to the United States as a gift.

People build monuments for events, too. In Washington, D.C., you can visit many of these national monuments. Some honor those who fought for freedom in wars. People can visit landmarks and monuments. They can learn why places, people, and events are important to our country.

The Statue of Liberty

Vietnam Veterans Memorial

4. **Explain** why national landmarks and monuments are important.

_____
_____
_____
_____
_____
_____

Got it?

TEKS 11.A, 11.B, 12.C

5. **Draw Conclusions** Why do citizens vote and pay taxes?

_____
_____
_____

6. Why should citizens tell leaders what services they need?

my Story Ideas

_____
_____
_____

7. Why is it important for communities to have police officers?

_____
_____
_____

Our Leaders

Envision It!

Circle the community leader in each picture.

TEKS
6.B, 12.A, 12.B, 12.C

Government leaders, or public officials, work to make our cities, states, and country better places to live. They help make laws. Good leaders should be honest and fair.

Community Leaders

The **mayor** is a government leader in a town or city. Mayors make decisions and solve problems. **Council** members are community citizens who work with the mayor. Some community leaders are appointed. Others are elected, or chosen, by the voters.

The mayor and the council make laws for a community. They work together to make sure that each neighborhood in a community has services it needs, such as schools, fire departments, and clean water.

TOWN COUNCIL

1. Work with a partner to name three public officials in your community, including the mayor.

40

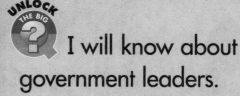
Vocabulary

mayor

council

governor

Draw a leader in your community.

State Leaders

The **governor** is the leader of a state. The governor works with other state leaders, such as representatives or senators. The citizens in each state elect their state leaders. Some state leaders are appointed.

The governor and other state leaders make laws that everyone in the state must follow. They decide how to spend money for the state. They might decide to open a state park or build a new highway.

Citizens vote for the governor.

2. ◉ **Main Idea and Details**
   Underline two ways that state leaders are selected.

3. Work with a partner to name the governor and one other public official in your state.

PEARSON realize Go online to access your interactive digital lesson.

41

The United States President

Citizens vote once every four years to choose our president, the leader of our country. The president's job is to sign new laws created by Congress and to make sure citizens follow laws. The president also nominates judges for the Supreme Court.

The president works in our country's capital in Washington, D.C. Every state has a capital, too.

4. Mark an X on our country's capital on the map below. Locate and (circle) Texas and its capital.

President Barack Obama in the Oval Office

United States Capitals

Comparing Public Officials

Mayor	Governor	President
Makes laws for the local community	Makes laws for the state	Makes sure people follow the country's laws
Makes decisions about using the community's money	Makes decisions about using the state's money	Makes decisions about using the country's money

Got it?

TEKS 12.A, 12.B

5. ◉ **Draw Conclusions** What problems does a mayor solve?

_____

_____

_____

_____

6. ? Compare the roles of a mayor, governor, and president.

 my Story Ideas

_____

_____

_____

_____

7. Work with a partner. Name the current president of the United States. Then name two other national public officials.

PEARSON realize. Go online to access your interactive digital lesson.

43

Our Country's Symbols

Envision It!

The United States flag is important to citizens.

TEKS
13.A, 14.A, 14.B, 14.C, 14.D, 18.E

The Pledge of Allegiance

I pledge allegiance to the flag of the United States of America and to the Republic for which it stands, one nation, under God, indivisible, with liberty and justice for all.

The United States has many symbols. A **symbol** is an object that stands for something else.

Our Country's Flag

Look at the picture of our country's flag on the right. There are 50 stars and 13 stripes on our country's flag. Each star stands for one of our 50 states. The stripes stand for the first 13 states. The people who created the flag were very inventive, or creative, to think of using stars and stripes!

We say the Pledge of Allegiance to show we are proud to be American citizens and to honor this symbol of freedom.

1. **Underline** why the flag shows creativity. **Say** the Pledge.

Vocabulary

symbol
anthem
motto
independence

Write two things you see on the flag.

Our Country's Songs

Our country has a national **anthem,** or song. This song is called "The Star Spangled Banner." It is about our flag. The last part of the song says the United States is "the land of the free and the home of the brave."

"America the Beautiful" is a song about the many beautiful places you can see in the United States. Another of our country's songs is "My Country, 'Tis of Thee." This song describes the United States as a "sweet land of liberty." It celebrates freedom in our country. We sing these songs to show we are proud to be Americans.

2. ◎ **Main Idea and Details**
Identify and **underline** the names of three of our country's patriotic songs.

The United States flag

The Great Seal of the United States and a penny both show symbols of our country.

More American Symbols

The bald eagle, which lives only in North America, is another symbol of our country. There is a picture of the bald eagle on The Great Seal of the United States. This seal also shows our country's motto. A **motto** is a saying that stands for an important idea. Our country's motto is *E pluribus unum*, or "Out of many, one." These words tell citizens that we are one country made up of different states and different people. Another symbol of our country is the rose. It was made our national flower in 1986. Uncle Sam is a symbol of our country, too. Uncle Sam is drawn as a man with white hair and a beard, and wearing a tall hat.

Long ago, a poster of Uncle Sam was used to ask men to fight for our country.

Our national flower, the rose

46

The poster of Uncle Sam shows him asking people to join the army. It shows that every individual can make a difference and contribute. It is a symbol of American individualism and inventiveness.

Some symbols, like the flag and the Liberty Bell, show our love of freedom. Long ago, the people who lived in America chose to fight for independence. **Independence** is freedom from being ruled by someone else. The Liberty Bell is now a symbol that celebrates that choice.

The Liberty Bell in Philadelphia, Pennsylvania

3. **Underline** a symbol that shows individualism.

 **Got it?**

TEKS 13.A, 14.C, 14.D, 18.E

4. ◉ **Main Idea and Details** **List** two symbols of our country.

_____

_____

_____

5. ❓ What do our country's symbols tell us about what is important to Americans?

my Story Ideas

_____

_____

_____

6. Which American symbols show our love of freedom?

_____

_____

TEKS Practice

Lesson 1

TEKS 13.A

1. **Write** one way you can be a good citizen at school.

Lesson 2

TEKS 13.A

2. **Draw** a picture showing a right that citizens have. **Fill in** the caption at the bottom of the picture.

Citizens have the right to

3. Look at the picture. **Draw** a person following a law.

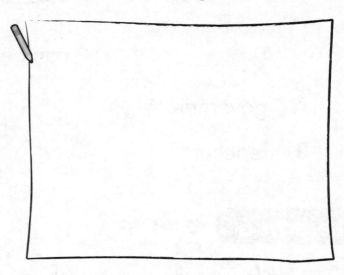

The law says we have to wear a seat belt when we are in a car.

4. ⊙ **Draw Conclusions** Why does the government want us to follow laws?

5. Explain why schools, libraries, parks, and fire stations are important to communities.

TEKS Practice

Lesson 5 TEKS 12.C

6. **Complete** the sentence. **Circle** the best choice.

A ________________ can be appointed or elected.

A government **C** state leader

B teacher **D** president

Lesson 6 TEKS 13.A

7. **List** four characteristics of good citizens.

8. **Draw** a symbol of the United States. **Label** your drawing.

Go online to write and illustrate your own **myStory Book** using the **myStory Ideas** from this chapter.

 ## How do people best cooperate?

TEKS

SS 20.A
ELA 17

In this chapter you have learned what it means to be a good citizen and to help others. You learned the role of the government and how government helps communities.

Think about your community. Is there a problem in your community? How could you fix it?

Draw a picture showing how you can cooperate with others to solve the problem. **Write** a caption.

PEARSON **realize** Go online to access your interactive digital lesson.

51

Working to Meet Our Needs

How do people get what they need?

Draw a picture of you and your family or friends having a meal together.

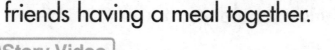

⭐ Texas Essential Knowledge and Skills

7.B Describe how natural resources and natural hazards affect activities and settlement patterns.

9.A Explain how work provides income to purchase goods and services.

9.B Explain the choices people in the U.S. free enterprise system can make about earning, spending, and saving money and where to live and work.

10.A Distinguish between producing and consuming.

10.B Identify ways in which people are both producers and consumers.

10.C Examine the development of a product from a natural resource to a finished product.

11.B Identify governmental services in the community such as police and fire protection, libraries, schools, and parks and explain their value to the community.

11.C Describe how governments tax citizens to pay for services.

18.D Sequence and categorize information.

18.E Interpret oral, visual, and print material by identifying the main idea, predicting, and comparing and contrasting.

19.B Create written and visual material such as stories, poems, maps, and graphic organizers to express ideas.

20.B Use a decision-making process to identify a situation that requires a decision, gather information, generate options, predict outcomes, take action to implement a decision, and reflect on the effectiveness of that decision.

 Begin With a Song

What We Buy

Sing to the tune of "Twinkle, Twinkle, Little Star."

All producers try and try,
To make things we want to buy.

Then they ship them to the store,
For consumers to explore.

A decision must be made,
Then the final bill gets paid.

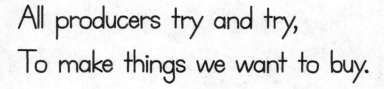

PEARSON realize   Go online to access your interactive digital lesson.

53

Vocabulary Preview

needs

wants

resource

cost

goods

producer

Identify examples of these words and (circle) them in the picture.

consumer

skill

trade

savings

borrow

loan

Needs and Wants

☐   ☐

Mark examples of things you must have to live with a ✓.

TEKS
9.A, 9.B

All people have needs and wants. **Needs** are things we must have to live. Food, clothing, and shelter are needs. **Wants** are things that we would like to have but do not need to live. How do we get the things we need and want?

Getting What We Need and Want

We use resources to get things we need and want. A **resource** is something that we can use. Some resources come from nature, like water and plants. Money is also a resource. Most people work to earn money to buy the goods and services they need and want.

1. **Look** at the photograph. **Write** N on a need and W on a want.

☐ ☐

Mark examples of things it would be nice to have with an X.

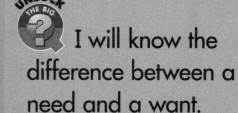
Vocabulary

needs   scarce

wants

resource

Making Choices

We cannot have everything we want. This is because resources are limited. For example, there is usually a limit to how much money we have. So, we often have to make choices. We have a free enterprise system. This means we can choose what we buy, or purchase. We can also choose the place or business where we buy goods or services.

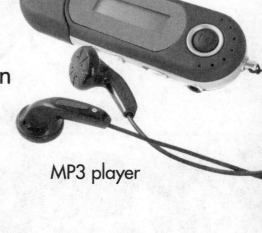

MP3 player

Carlos likes music. He wants to learn to play the harmonica. He also wants an MP3 player. Carlos will have to choose between buying the harmonica and the MP3 player. He does not have enough money to buy both.

2. **Look** at the photographs. (Circle) what you would choose. **Tell** a partner why.

Harmonica

PEARSON realize | Go online to access your interactive digital lesson.

57

Families Make Choices

Families have to make choices about their needs and wants, too. Sometimes, resources are scarce. **Scarce** means there is not enough of something.

Families take care of the things they need first. What kind of food is best for us? Which clothes will keep us warm and dry? Where will we live and work? For each need, they can make choices about what they buy or where they live or work.

Then families make choices about what they want. If they want games, they can choose from many different games in a store.

3. ◉ **Draw Conclusions Write** a sentence about the choice the family in the picture is making.

Communities Make Choices

People in a community make choices about how to use natural resources. People in this picture will decide how to use this school land. They will choose to plant a garden or build a playground. There is not enough land to do both.

4. **Circle** the area in the picture that shows the resource that is scarce.

TEKS 9.A, 9.B

5. 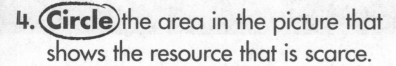 **Main Idea and Details** In a free enterprise system, what choices can families make to meet their needs?

_____

_____

_____

_____

6. **List** two wants that you would like to buy. **my Story Ideas**

_____

_____

7. How do people get money to pay for goods and services?

_____

_____

_____

_____

PEARSON realize   Go online to access your interactive digital lesson.

59

Making Good Choices

Circle the two items you would buy.

TEKS
9.B, 18.E, 20.B

People and communities make choices every day about how to use resources. How do they decide which choice is best? Let's see how some choices are made.

What Is the Choice?

The Archer family has money to spend on a family activity. First, they talk about things they like to do. Then they list two choices or options.

The Archers will visit the science center or buy a new board game. They have enough money to pay for only one of these things. How will they decide which to choose?

1. ◎ **Cause and Effect Underline** the reason the Archers will make a choice.

Vocabulary

benefit

cost

Tell a partner why you chose the items.

Steps for Making Choices

First, the Archers will talk about the benefits of each choice. A **benefit** is a good result from a choice you make. At the science center, the Archers can learn about how things work and do fun experiments. If they buy a game, the game can last for a long time. It can be shared with friends, too.

Next, the family will talk about the costs of each choice. The **cost** is the price of something. The science center tickets cost $48. The game costs $35.

Then, after thinking about the benefits and costs, they will make their choice. What would you choose?

2. **Write** 1, 2, or 3 next to each paragraph above to show the order of the steps.

Benefits and Costs

The Archers made a chart to help them compare their choices. A chart can help you make a decision. It shows information clearly. The Archers listed the costs and benefits of each choice.

3. Read the benefits. **Mark** an X in the box for the activity you would choose.

What Should We Choose?			
Activity	Benefits	Cost	Choice
Family Game	1. Can use the game for a long time 2. Can share the game with friends	$35	☐
Science Center	1. Will learn how things work 2. Can do experiments	$48	☐

Making the Decision

The Archers chose the science center. They used computers to learn about floods and tornadoes. These events happen where the Archers live, so it was a good decision to learn about them.

4. **Underline** the reason the Archers thought they made a good decision.

Got it?

TEKS 9.B, 20.B

5. **Main Idea and Details** What is one idea you can think about before you make a choice?

_____

_____

_____

6.  You have enough money to go to the movies or to buy a book. **Circle** your choice. **Write** a benefit of your choice.

my Story Ideas

_____

_____

_____

_____

7. On a separate sheet of paper, **list** two things you might buy. **Find out** the cost and benefits of each. **Circle** the one you would most like to buy. Why is this the best choice?

Producing and Consuming Goods

Look at the pictures of the baker making pretzels.

TEKS
7.B, 9.B, 10.A, 10.B, 18.E

This farmer sells tomatoes. The money she gets is her income.

Goods are things that people make or grow. Your family uses and buys goods. Goods are everything from tomatoes to televisions to trucks!

A person who makes or grows goods is a **producer.** A person who buys and uses goods is a **consumer.**

1. **Look** at the photograph. **Write** a P on the producer and a C on the consumer.

Producing Goods

People produce goods to earn money. Money that people earn is called **income.** Income is used to buy things people need and want.

Draw what happens next.

Deciding What to Produce

Producers grow or make goods that consumers want to buy. Read about Farmer Green.

Farmer Green grows berries. She must decide if she should grow strawberries or blueberries. She learns that there are already a lot of blueberry farms in her community. Consumers can buy blueberries easily. There are not many strawberry farms.

People in her community will probably buy strawberries from Farmer Green if they cannot buy them from other producers. She will be able to sell a lot of strawberries at a good price.

2. ◎ **Main Idea and Details** **Underline** a detail that tells why Farmer Green might decide to grow strawberries instead of blueberries.

PEARSON realize   Go online to access your interactive digital lesson.

65

Natural Resources

A natural resource is something useful that comes from the earth. Air, water, sunlight, and soil are all natural resources. Farmer Green needs soil and water to grow her strawberries.

3. **Underline** the definition of *natural resource.*

Other Kinds of Resources

Farmer Green needs other kinds of resources, too. She needs money and farm equipment. They are called capital resources. The tractor shown is a capital resource. She needs people to help plant and pick the strawberries. Workers are called human resources. Farmer Green needs natural, capital, and human resources to grow and sell strawberries.

Workers pick the strawberries when they are ripe. Then they put them on a truck that carries them to a market. Farmer Green, the producer, earns money selling the berries. The consumer buys the strawberries. Everyone gets something they want!

4. **Underline** two ways human resources are helpful on Farmer Green's farm.

 **Got it?**

 TEKS 10.A, 10.B

5. ◉ **Main Idea and Details List** three kinds of resources.

_____

_____

6. ? **Describe** a place you go to buy food.   my Story Ideas

_____

_____

_____

7. **List** three kinds of producers. **List** three products you consume.

_____

_____

_____

Reading a Flowchart

A flowchart shows the order or sequence in which things happen. Some flowcharts show a process. Each box shows a step in the process. Each arrow points to the next step.

Read the title of the flowchart below. The flowchart shows producers picking and squeezing oranges, and then consumers buying the juice.

Point to the first step. Tell what happens first. Follow the arrow with your finger. Tell what happens next. Follow the arrow with your finger. What is happening in the last step?

How We Get Orange Juice

Producers grow oranges in orchards. They pick them when they are ripe.

Oranges are squeezed at a factory. Juice goes into cartons.

Trucks bring cartons of juice to stores. Consumers buy the juice.

TEKS

SS 10.C Examine the development of a product from a natural resource to a finished product.

SS 18.D Sequence and categorize information.

SS 19.B Create visual material such as graphic organizers to express ideas.

Try it!

1. **Circle** the word that tells where oranges are made into juice.

   factory   store   orchard

2. **Complete** the sentence. A flowchart shows the

   _____

   _____ in which things happen.

3. **Draw** pictures on the flowchart. Add steps that show a family eating and cleaning up. **Mark** an arrow between the boxes to show the sequence.

Having Dinner Together

PEARSON realize Go online to access your interactive digital lesson.

69

Service Workers and Their Jobs

Look at the photographs. These people help others in their community.

TEKS
11.B, 11.C

Services are jobs that people do to help others. People who do these jobs are called service workers.

Services in the Community

In every community, many people work to provide, or give, services. Police officers, school nurses, and librarians are all service workers. Service workers are often paid for the services they do.

Taxi drivers, truck drivers, and street sweepers all provide services on our roads. Can you think of other people who provide services in your community?

1. **Write** three services provided in your community.

_____

_____

A road crew provides a service by fixing our roads.

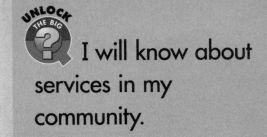

Draw a picture of someone who helps people in your community.

Special Skills

Doctors and nurses provide an important service. They help people stay healthy. They help people who are sick to get better.

Doctors and nurses need special skills to help people. A **skill** is knowing how to do something. Doctors need to know how to use special equipment to listen to people's hearts. They also use equipment to look inside people's ears and to weigh people.

Many doctors specialize in one area. To **specialize** means to do one kind of thing very well. We visit some doctors for problems with our eyes, and other doctors when we break a bone.

2. <u>Underline</u> a special skill above.

PEARSON
realize | Go online to access your interactive digital lesson.

71

Other Service Workers

We also have service workers in our schools. Principals, nurses, librarians, cafeteria workers, janitors, and teachers work in our schools. These service workers all have skills that help them do their jobs.

Some teachers specialize in one subject like math, history, or reading. Other teachers have to know how to teach music or physical education.

3. **Write** the name of a worker at your school who specializes in one area.

_____

- - - - - - - - - - - - - - - - - -

_____

Government Workers

Police officers and firefighters are government workers. Communities pay these workers with money from taxes. A tax is money collected by a government to pay for services. Government leaders such as mayors, governors, and even our president are paid from taxes, too.

People who work for the post office are government workers, too. They work hard to make sure people all over the United States receive mail.

4.  **Main Idea and Details**
   Underline three government workers.

🔻 TEKS 11.B, 11.C

5. ◎ **Draw Conclusions** What is one reason it is important for some workers to have special skills?

_____

_____

_____

6. ❓ How do we pay for community services?  my Story Ideas

_____

_____

7. Why are government and other service workers important in your community?

_____

_____

_____

_____

Main Idea and Details

When you read a paragraph, or listen to someone speak, look and listen for the main idea and details. The main idea tells you what the information is about. Details tell you more about the main idea.

Read the letter below. The main idea is circled. The details are underlined.

Dear Mr. Patel,

(I really liked art class this year.)
I liked making pots with clay. It was fun finger painting. Making flowers with tissue paper was my favorite. Thank you for being a great teacher.

Sincerely,

Susan Lester

Learning Objective

I will know how to identify the main idea and details in a paragraph.

TEKS

SS 18.E Interpret oral and print material by identifying the main idea.

ELA 14.A Identify the main idea in a text and distinguish it from the topic.

Read the letter aloud with a partner.

Dear Susan,

You are a talented art student. Your clay pot will make a nice gift. Your finger painting was very colorful. Your tissue paper flowers were lovely. Thank you for your kind letter. Keep making great art!

Sincerely,

Mr. Patel

Underline three details. **Write** the main idea you hear.

_____

- -

_____

PEARSON realize Go online to access your interactive digital lesson.

75

Trading for Goods and Services

Envision It!

Circle the goods in the photograph that the children trade.

TEKS
7.B, 9.B, 10.A, 10.B

How do we get the goods and services we need and want? We trade for them. **Trade** means to buy, sell, or exchange goods or services with someone else. Any place we trade for goods or services is called a market.

Trading Goods

When you go to the store, you probably use money to pay for the things you want. Long ago, people did not use money to buy things. They bartered goods to get what they needed. To **barter** is to trade goods or services without using money. Today, some people barter, but most people use money to buy what they need.

1. **Main Idea and Details** **Underline** a detail about trading goods.

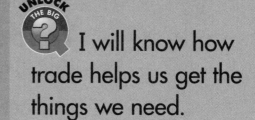

Draw something that you and a friend might trade with each other.

Supply and Demand

Producers make choices about what to sell. They think about **demand,** or how many consumers want a good. Then they think about **supply,** or how much there is. Supply and demand help producers decide how much they can charge for their product.

Pat loves to eat fish, but she lives in a city that is not near water. Not many places near Pat's home sell fish. A lot of people want this natural resource, so the people who sell it can charge a high price.

Pat's grandmother lives by the ocean. When Pat visits her, she gets to eat a lot of fish. Producers who sell fish cannot charge a high price or people would buy from someone else.

2. **Underline** two reasons why fish costs more in Pat's city.

PEARSON
realize   Go online to access your
           interactive digital lesson.   77

Trade in the United States

People in one state can trade goods with people in other states. Oranges grow in Florida. The winters there are warm. Soybeans grow in Iowa. The soil there is rich. So, producers in Florida can sell oranges to consumers in Iowa. Producers in Iowa can sell soybeans to consumers in Florida.

3. **Look** at the map. **Write** one way for consumers in Illinois to get oranges.

_____

- - - - - - - - - - - - - - - - -

_____

_____

- - - - - - - - - - - - - - - - -

_____

United States Trade

Legend
- major orange-producing state
- major soybean-producing state

Trade With Other Countries

Some goods and services that people in the United States use are not produced here. We can trade with other countries to get those things. There are not many places in the United States where bananas grow well. The bananas you eat might come from Ecuador.

4. **Underline** a country that trades with the United States.

 Got it?

🔻 TEKS 9.B, 10.B

5. ◉ **Main Idea and Details** What is the main idea of why people trade?

_____

_____

_____

_____

6. ⓺ Where does your family choose to buy things you need and want?

 my Story Ideas

_____

_____

7. Why does the United States trade with other countries?

_____

_____

Making Choices About Money

START TO SAVE TODAY!

My Savings

Write an S on the picture that shows someone saving money.

TEKS
9.A, 9.B, 18.E

Have you ever earned money or received it as a gift? What did you do with that money? Did you spend it right away? Did you save it to buy something later? **Save** means to keep something to use later.

Why Do People Save?

Meet Yoshi. Yoshi walks his neighbor's dog once a week. His neighbor pays him two dollars for doing this job.

Yoshi does not spend the money he earns right away. He saves his money to buy a game. Every week, Yoshi puts his money in a piggy bank.

1. **Write** something you would like to save for.

_____

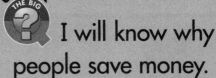 I will know why people save money.

Vocabulary

save

savings

borrow

loan

Write an SP on the picture that shows someone spending money.

A Savings Plan

The money in Yoshi's piggy bank is called savings. **Savings** is money that you do not spend right away. When Yoshi has enough savings, he will buy the game.

Yoshi has a chart to show his savings plan. The main idea of a savings plan is to set goals for how much money to save. If Yoshi saves the money he earns each week, he predicts he will be able to buy the game.

The game Yoshi wants costs $8. Look at Yoshi's savings plan. Yoshi's savings plan shows that if he saves all of his money from walking dogs, he will be able to buy the game in four weeks.

Yoshi's Savings Plan

Week	Saved
Week 1	$2
Week 2	$2
Week 3	$2
Week 4	$2
Total =	

2. Using the chart as a visual, **interpret** what Yoshi will save over time. **Predict** what Yoshi might buy if he saved for four more weeks.

Kate's grandfather helps
her open a savings
account.

Saving at a Bank

Yoshi's friend Kate is also saving
money. Kate earns money by raking
her neighbor's yard. She wants to save
her money. Her grandfather took her
to a bank to open a savings account.
A savings account is money saved in a
bank. It will not get lost or stolen. Kate's
money is safe in the bank.

3. ⊙ **Draw Conclusions**
   <u>**Underline**</u> one reason that people
   save money at a bank.

Borrowing Money

Sometimes people need to buy
something right away but do not have
enough money. They may decide to
borrow money from a bank. **Borrow**
means to use something now and give
it back later. When people borrow
money, that money is called a **loan.**
They will need to pay back the loan at
a later time.

Sometimes Kate's
grandfather uses a credit
card to buy things.

People can also get credit cards from a
bank to buy things. Using a credit card
is the same as getting a loan.

Sometimes Kate's grandfather uses a credit card to buy things. Kate's grandfather will pay the credit card bill at the end of the month. The bank will get back the money it loaned.

4. **Fill in** the blank. Money you borrow is called a _____

Got it?

TEKS 9.A, 9.B, 18.E

5. **Main Idea and Details Explain** why people save their money.

_____

_____

_____

_____

6. What could you buy if you saved for a long time? How would you save the money?

my Story Ideas

_____

_____

_____

_____

7. **Write** an item that you want and its cost. How could you earn the money to buy it? How long would it take you?

_____

_____

_____

_____

Lesson 1 TEKS 9.B

1. **Read** the question and (circle) the best answer.

   Which item below is a want?

   A shoes

   B cell phone

   C apple

   D water

2. **Write** two choices you could make when buying this item.

_____

_____

_____

Lesson 2 TEKS 20.B

3. A box of markers costs $8. A new T-shirt costs $17. **Write** the item you would choose and a benefit for your choice.

_____

_____

_____

4. ◉ **Main Idea and Details** Why do producers need to sell things that consumers will buy?

_____

_____

_____

5. **Look** at the pictures. **Write** _yes_ if the picture shows a government service, or _no_ if it does not.

_____   _____   _____

Lesson 5  TEKS 10.B

6. **Circle** the picture that shows bartering. **Underline** the picture that shows people using money to trade.

7. How are the people in the picture on the left both producers and consumers?

_____

_____

_____

Lesson 6  TEKS 9.B

8. Why do people save money?

_____

_____

_____

_____

Go online to write and illustrate your own **myStory Book** using the **myStory Ideas** from this chapter.

How do people get what they need?

TEKS

SS 9.A, 9.B, 10.A, 10.B
ELA 17

In this chapter you have learned about how people provide goods and services. You also learned how people are able to get those goods and services.

What is a good or service you would like to provide to earn income when you grow up?

Draw a picture that shows you selling a good or providing a service. Include the people or consumers who are buying your goods or using your service. **Write** a caption for your picture.

The World Around Us

my Story Spark

What is the world like?

Draw a picture of the place where you live.

my Story Video

⭐ Texas Essential Knowledge and Skills

5.A Interpret information on maps and globes using basic map elements such as title, orientation (north, south, east, west), and legend/map keys.

5.B Create maps to show places and routes within the home, school, and community.

6.A Identify major landforms and bodies of water, including each of the continents and each of the oceans, on maps and globes.

6.B Locate places of significance, including the local community, Texas, the state capital, the U.S. capital, major cities in Texas, the coast of Texas, Canada, Mexico, and the United States on maps and globes.

6.C Examine information from various sources about places and regions.

7.A Describe how weather patterns and seasonal patterns affect activities and settlement patterns.

7.B Describe how natural resources and natural hazards affect activities and settlement patterns.

7.C Explain how people depend on the physical environment and natural resources to meet basic needs.

7.D Identify the characteristics of different communities, including urban, suburban, and rural, and how they affect activities and settlement patterns.

8.A Identify ways in which people have modified the physical environment such as building roads, clearing land for urban development and agricultural use, and drilling for oil.

8.B Identify positive and negative consequences of human modification of the physical environment such as the use of irrigation to improve crop yields.

8.C Identify ways people can conserve and replenish natural resources.

18.B Obtain information about a topic using a variety of valid visual sources such as pictures, maps, electronic sources, literature, reference sources, and artifacts.

18.E Interpret oral, visual, and print material by identifying the main idea, predicting, and comparing and contrasting.

19.B Create written and visual material such as stories, poems, maps, and graphic organizers to express ideas.

Begin With a Song

Places Where We Live

by Charlotte Munez

Sing to the tune of "On Top of Old Smokey."

We live in big cities
And suburbs or towns.
These places are different
In their sights and their sounds.

Big cities and small towns
Are found everywhere.
A road or a highway
Will take you right there!

PEARSON realize Go online to access your interactive digital lesson.

89

Vocabulary Preview

- symbol
- continent
- ocean
- landform
- weather
- environment

rural

natural resource

renewable

conserve

technology

transportation

Talking About Location

☐ ☐

Mark the picture of the bird under a branch with an **X**.

TEKS
5.B, 6.B, 6.C, 18.E

Look around. What do you see? Everything around you is in a certain location, or place. Location tells where something is.

Relative Location

Are you sitting near or far from the door to your classroom? **Relative location** tells where something is by comparing it to something else. Location words like *above, below, next to, near,* and *far* tell the relative location of people, places, and things.

1. **Underline** the location words on this page.

Bakery 10

Rainbow Restaurant 12 Open

Main Street 14

UNLOCK THE BIG ? I will know how to talk about location.

Vocabulary
....
relative location
absolute location

Mark the picture of the bird above a branch with a ✓.

Absolute Location

How does a postal worker know where to deliver a letter? The address on a letter tells the absolute location of a place, such as a home or school. An **absolute location** is the exact spot where a place is located. A postal worker uses absolute location to make sure that every letter is delivered to the right place.

2. ◉ **Main Idea and Details Look** at the Rainbow Restaurant in the picture. **Write** the absolute location of the Rainbow Restaurant.

_____

_____

Maps Show Places and Routes

A map shows what a place looks like from above. You can create a map to show places within the home, school, or community. You can include a number of elements on a map you create. These include symbols, a legend, and a compass rose.

The map below shows the community of Washington, D.C. The purple line shows the route, or path, from the Capitol to the White House. To show a route on a map you create, you locate the start and end points. Then mark the route between the two locations.

Washington, D.C.

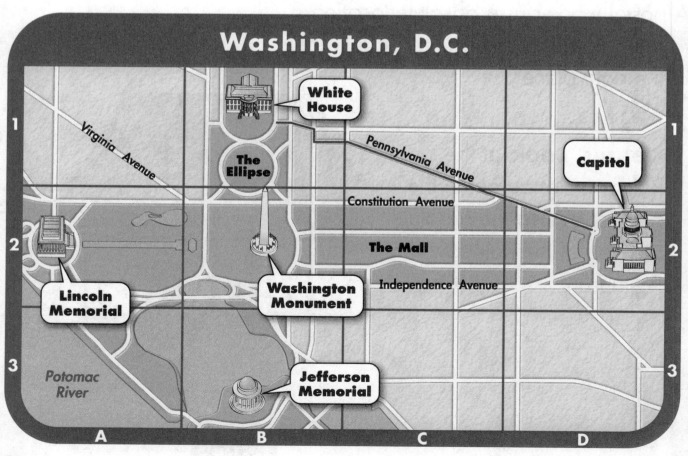

3. Trace the route between the Capitol and the White House. **Name** one street on the route.

_____

- -

_____

4. Draw a line to **create a route** from the Capitol to the Lincoln Memorial.

Got it?

TEKS 5.B, 6.C, 18.E

5. ◎ **Compare and Contrast** Compare and contrast absolute location and relative location.

_____

- -

_____

- -

_____

6. **?** **Write** a relative location for your desk.   my Story Ideas

_____

- -

_____

7. On a separate sheet of paper, **draw** a map to show the locations of your home and school. Then draw the route you take from your home to your school.

All About Maps

Look at the mountain.
Draw a simple shape to show the mountain.

TEKS
5.A, 5.B, 6.C, 19.B

Maps can show many different things. A map can show natural things, such as land and water. A map can also show things that people have put on the land, such as roads and buildings. It can show a route, or path.

Why We Use Maps

The family in the photograph is using a map to follow a trail or path. The map also shows which direction to go to find the closest picnic area.

1. **Draw** a simple map of your classroom. **Draw** a route from the door to your desk.

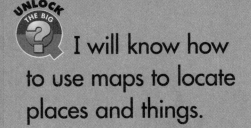
Vocabulary

symbol
cardinal direction
intermediate direction

Draw a map of your home. Use simple shapes to show rooms and furniture.

Using the Parts of a Map

The map title tells the main idea of a map. This map uses pictures to stand for real things. These pictures are called **symbols.** The legend, or key, tells what each symbol means.

2. **Draw** a line from each legend symbol to its location on the map. Then **draw** the route from the ranger station to the picnic area.

Rock Trail

Legend

walking path
river
entrance
picnic area
ranger station

PEARSON realize Go online to access your interactive digital lesson.

97

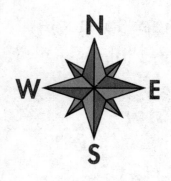

Cardinal and Intermediate Directions

A compass rose shows directions. It uses letters to stand for directions. **Cardinal directions** are the four main directions. These are north, south, east, and west. In between these are intermediate directions, northeast, southeast, southwest, and northwest.

3. ◉ **Main Idea and Details Look** at the map and use the compass rose. **Write** an *N* on the place that is north of Town Hall. **Circle** the place that is west of Town Hall. **Underline** the map's main idea.

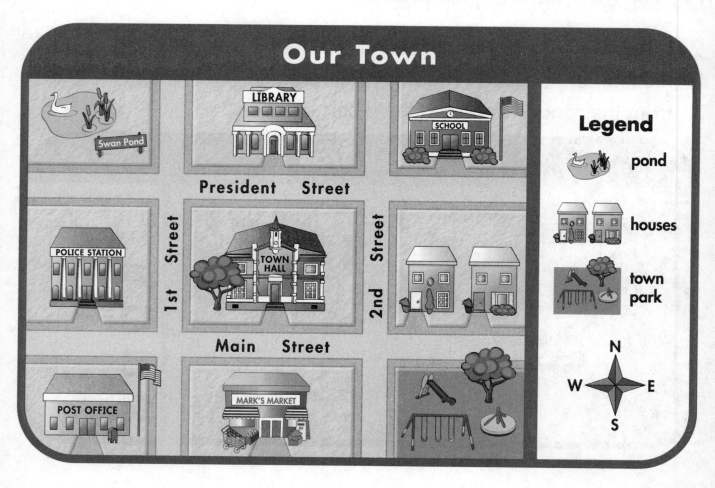

Maps of Home and School

You can use the things you have learned about maps to create your own maps. You can create a map to show places and routes within a home. A map of your home might show rooms like a kitchen or bedroom. You could use symbols for stairways or a stove to create your map legend. You can show a route from the kitchen to your bedroom.

You can also create a map of places and routes within a school. A map of your school could show the library and the principal's office. You can use symbols like exits or classrooms. You can also show a route from your classroom to the main office.

TEKS 5.B, 19.B

4. ◉ **Draw Conclusions** Why do people use maps?

_____

_____

5. **List** something natural and something made by humans that you pass on the route to your school.

_____

_____

6. On a separate sheet of paper, **create** a map of a bedroom you would like to have. Use symbols to show where your bed, door, and other objects would be. **Draw** a line showing the route from your bed to the door.

Using a Map Scale

A map is smaller than the real area on Earth it shows. You can use a map scale to figure out the distance, or amount of space, between two places. Look at the scale on this map of Texas. If you put a ruler under the scale, you will see that 1 inch stands for about 200 miles. The green part at the top of the scale is half the length of the bar, or half the distance. The green part represents 100 miles.

Texas, Political

| 0 | 200 mi |
| 0 | 200 km |

Amarillo

Oklahoma

New Mexico

Arkansas

Lubbock

Plano   Garland

Irving

Dallas

Abilene   Ft. Worth   Arlington

Louisiana

Waco

Austin ★   Beaumont

Houston

MEXICO

San Antonio   Pasadena

Legend
★ state capital
• city

Laredo   • Corpus Christi

Gulf of Mexico

Brownsville

Learning Objective

I will know how to identify and use a map scale and legend.

TEKS

SS 5.A Interpret information on maps using basic map elements.
SS 5.B Create maps to show places and routes within the community.
SS 6.C Examine information from various sources about places and regions.
ELA 25.C Record basic information in simple visual formats.

Follow the steps for using a map scale and legend.

- Look at the legend to find the symbol for a city. Place a strip of paper from the dot by San Antonio to the dot by Pasadena. Mark each dot on the strip of paper.

- Place the strip of paper along the map scale with one mark at zero.

- The other mark is at 200. That means the distance between San Antonio and Pasadena is about 200 miles.

Try it!

1. Use the scale to **measure** the distance in miles between Amarillo and Lubbock.

   _____

   - - - - - - - - - - - - - - - - - -

   _____

2. **Create** a simple map of an area in your community. Include buildings, roads, and parks on your map. **Draw** a line showing the route between two places.

PEARSON realize Go online to access your interactive digital lesson.

101

Our Earth

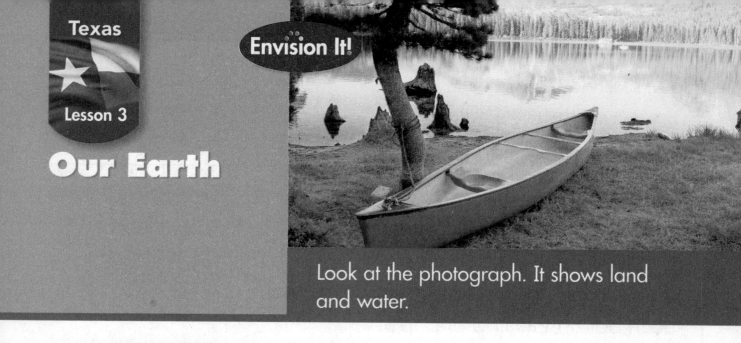

Look at the photograph. It shows land and water.

TEKS
5.A, 6.A, 6.B, 6.C, 18.E

Earth has seven large areas of land called **continents.** They are North America, South America, Europe, Africa, Asia, Australia, and Antarctica. Earth has four bodies of water called **oceans** that cover most of its surface. They are the Atlantic Ocean, Pacific Ocean, Indian Ocean, and Arctic Ocean.

Earth's Shape

This illustration shows part of Earth. You can see that Earth's shape is round, like a ball. Earth is very large. Because of Earth's shape, illustrations and even photographs taken from space can only show one part of Earth at a time.

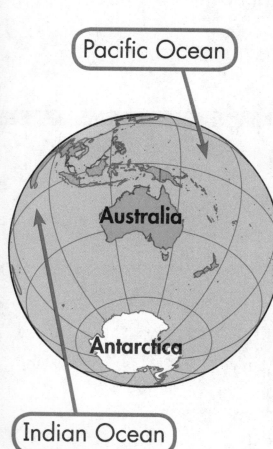

1. ◎ **Cause and Effect** <u>Underline</u> the reason you cannot view all of Earth at one time.

Draw another picture that shows land and water.

 I will know how Earth is shown on a globe and on a world map.

Vocabulary

continent
ocean
equator
prime meridian

Showing Earth on a Globe

One way to learn about something large is to look at a model, or small copy, of the real thing. A globe is a model of Earth that shows its continents and oceans.

Look at the North and South Poles on the picture of a globe. It is very cold in both of these locations. Look for the equator. The **equator** is an imaginary line that divides Earth in half. The northern half is called the Northern Hemisphere. The southern half is called the Southern Hemisphere. People who live in the United States live in the Northern Hemisphere.

2. **Write** the letter *N* on the Northern Hemisphere, and the letter *S* on the Southern Hemisphere. With a partner, use a globe to locate both hemispheres.

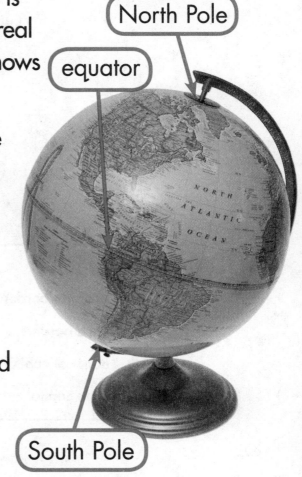

North Pole

equator

South Pole

Using Globes

You can use a globe to find locations of places. A globe has tools that can help you find out more about places. Like maps, some globes have a compass rose. A compass shows which way is north, south, east, and west. On a globe you can identify each of the continents and major bodies of water, including oceans. You can use the globes on pages 102 and 106 to identify each of the continents and major bodies of water, including oceans.

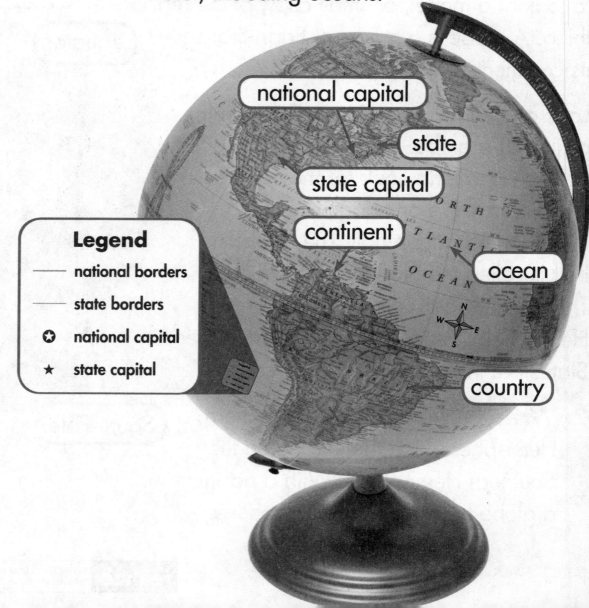

national capital

state

state capital

continent

ocean

country

Legend
— national borders
— state borders
⊛ national capital
★ state capital

A legend can help you identify land, water, capitals, and borders. Borders are the imaginary lines that divide countries and states. Look at the symbol for borders on the legend to the right. This picture of a globe shows the borders between the United States, Canada, and Mexico. Globes also show continents and oceans.

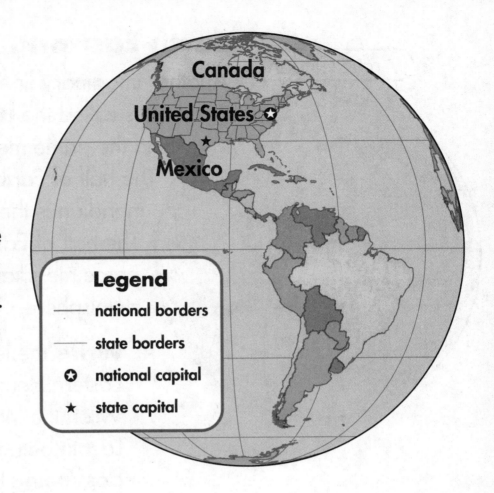

Legend
— national borders
— state borders
⊛ national capital
★ state capital

You can use the legend to find capitals. Look for the star symbols on the legend. There is one for state capitals and one for national, or country, capitals. Notice how they are different.

3. **Draw** a circle around the capital of the United States.

   With a partner, use a classroom globe to locate the United States, Canada, Mexico, and the capital of the United States.

Earth East and West

Another imaginary line that divides Earth in half is called the **prime meridian.** Find the prime meridian on the globe. The half of Earth east of the prime meridian is the Eastern Hemisphere. The half of Earth west of the prime meridian is the Western Hemisphere.

4. **Write** the letter *E* on the Eastern Hemisphere and the letter *W* on the Western Hemisphere. Locate both hemispheres on a classroom globe.

Latitude and Longitude

A world map is a flat drawing of Earth. Mapmakers use a special grid system that helps us find the exact location of any place on Earth. This system uses two sets of imaginary lines called lines of latitude and lines of longitude.

Lines that run east and west are lines of latitude. Lines that run north and south are lines of longitude.

5. **Write** what kind of line the equator is.

_____

_____

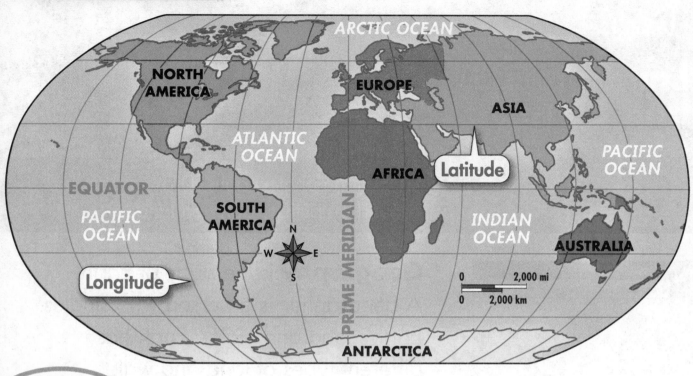

Got it?

⬇ TEKS 5.A, 6.A, 18.E

6. ◉ **Main Idea and Details Write** one relative location of North America.

_____

- -

_____

7. ? **Identify** which ocean is closest to your home.

my Story Ideas

_____

- -

8. Circle each of the continents on the map above. **Underline** all the names of the oceans. Then identify the continents, oceans, major bodies of water, and landforms on a classroom globe with a partner.

PEARSON
realize   Go online to access your
interactive digital lesson.   **107**

Landforms and Bodies of Water

Look at the photographs. Draw a box around an activity done on land.

TEKS
6.A, 6.B, 6.C

Geography is the study of Earth. A geographer is a person who studies Earth's land and water. Earth has different types of land and water.

Landforms

The shapes of Earth's land are called **landforms.** A mountain is the highest land on Earth. A hill is an area of raised land. It is like a mountain, but it is not as high. The low land between mountains or hills is called a valley.

A plain is a large area of flat land. Plains do not have big hills or mountains. A high plain is called a plateau. Plateaus are far above the level of the ocean.

1. ◉ **Draw Conclusions** Write *mountain* and *plain* on the landforms in the photograph.

Vocabulary

geography
landform
physical map
political map

Circle an activity done on water.

Bodies of Water

Earth has two kinds of water, salt water and fresh water. Oceans have salt water. Rivers and lakes have fresh water. A river is a long body of water that flows into another body of water. A lake is a body of water surrounded by land.

2. **Underline** two kinds of water.

Land Meets Water

An island is a landform that has water on all sides. A peninsula has water on all sides but one. The place where land meets the ocean is called the coast.

3. **Write** a landform shown in the photograph.

_____

_____

PEARSON
realize   Go online to access your interactive digital lesson.

109

Physical Maps

Physical maps show Earth's continents and bodies of water. The colors and symbols on a physical map show landforms, rivers, lakes, and oceans. The color blue is used to show water.

The physical map below shows major landforms and bodies of water around the world. Continents are labeled in black. Oceans and major rivers and lakes are labeled in blue.

4. (Circle) the major world rivers on this map. Underline two large lakes. Identify major bodies of water, including each of the oceans.

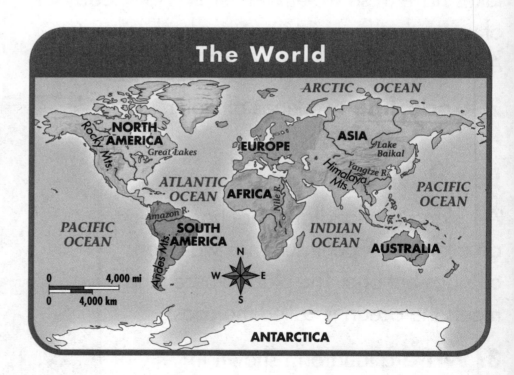

The World

Political Maps

Political maps show imaginary lines called borders. Towns, states, and countries all have borders. Look at the political map of North America. It shows the borders of the countries in North America.

5. (Circle) a border line on the map.

CANADA

PACIFIC OCEAN

UNITED STATES

ATLANTIC OCEAN

Gulf of Mexico

MEXICO

Caribbean Islands

Central America

0   1,500 mi
0   1,500 km

N W E S

TEKS 6.B, 6.C

6. ⊙ **Main Idea and Details** (Circle) the countries and regions in North America on the map above.

7. **Write** the name of one landform or body of water located in your community.

my Story Ideas

_____

_____

8. **Write** the kinds of maps you would use to locate Austin, Texas, and the Gulf of Mexico.

_____

_____

Weather and Climate

Envision It!

Draw something you can use when it rains.

TEKS
6.C, 7.A, 7.B

What is the weather today? **Weather** is what it is like outside at a certain time and place. Does the air feel cold or hot? We use the word **temperature** to talk about how hot or cold something is.

Wet and Dry Weather

Weather can also be wet or dry. Wet days are cloudy, with rain or snow. Snow falls when it is cold outside. On dry days, there is no rain or snow. Dry days are often sunny and clear. Clear means there are no clouds.

When the weather is cold and wet, we choose warm clothes. When the weather is hot and dry, we choose light clothes.

1. ◉ **Cause and Effect** (Circle) clues in the photo that tell what the weather is like. **Write** one word to describe

the weather: _____

Draw something you can use when it snows.

UNLOCK THE BIG ?

I will know how different kinds of weather affect people, animals, and plants.

Vocabulary

weather   climate
temperature   region

Weather and Nature

Animals and plants live and grow in different places. Polar bears are animals that live only where the weather is cold. Their heavy fur helps them stay warm in places that are cold and snowy.

Moss is a plant that grows in places where the weather is wet. A rainforest is a place with very wet weather. It can rain 14 feet in one year! Wet weather is good for frogs. It keeps their skin from getting too dry.

2. **Underline** how wet weather helps frogs.

Many frogs live in the Hoh Rainforest in Washington State.

PEARSON realize Go online to access your interactive digital lesson.

113

Climate Regions

The weather a place has over a long time is called its **climate.** Climate patterns affect the way people live. People who live in a cold, snowy climate often wear warm clothes and boots. For fun, they might ski and sled.

A **region** is an area that shares something alike. Some regions share the same climate. The map below shows five different climate regions in the United States.

3. Outline Texas's climate regions on the map. Circle your climate on the legend.

United States Climate Regions

Legend
- marine
- cold
- warm and wet
- hot and wet
- hot and dry

Weather Changes

Weather changes every day. Sudden weather changes can be dangerous. A lot of rain can cause a flood. Weather with strong winds is called a storm. Tornadoes and hurricanes are both dangerous kinds of storms. People may need to leave their homes to be safe.

Tornado

4. **Underline** two dangerous storms.

🔻 TEKS 6.C, 7.A, 7.B

5. **Predict** **Interpret** the printed material at the top of the page. **Predict** what would happen if a tornado or a hurricane hit your hometown.

_____

_____

_____

_____

6. ❓ What is the weather in your region today?   my Story Ideas

_____

_____

7. What does a climate region map show you?

_____

_____

Our Environment

Think about how this area is the same as or different from where you live.

TEKS
7.C, 7.D, 8.A, 8.B, 8.C, 18.E

The **environment** is the air, land, water, and life around us. It is the plants, animals, people, and buildings that make up where we live. People choose to change the environment they live in to get things they need.

People Change the Land

People build cities on the land. A city is an **urban** environment. Most cities start small and grow. In cities, people build highways, apartment buildings, and office buildings.

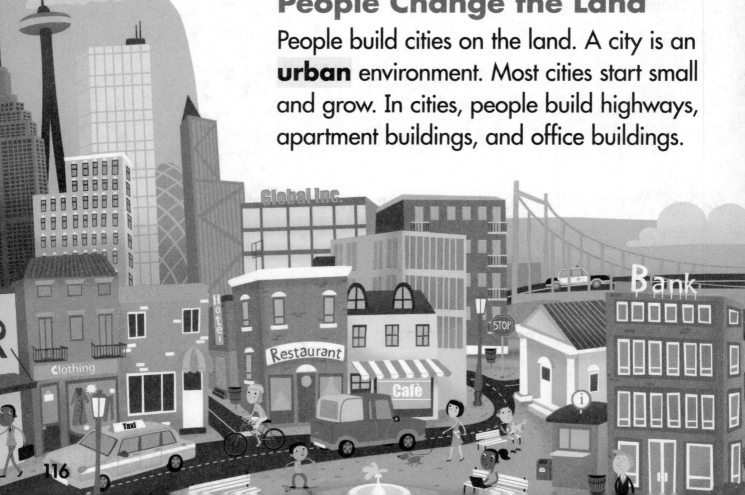

Draw a picture of where you live.

UNLOCK THE BIG ?

I will know ways that people change their environment.

Vocabulary

environment   rural

urban   natural

suburban   resource

Before building, people remove the trees and other plants. Animals must find other places to live. People use machines to make the land flat.

A **suburban** environment is close to a city. In the suburbs, people clear land to build roads, houses, parks, and shopping centers. A **rural** environment is made up of small towns and farms. Farmers clear land to plant crops.

1. ◎ **Compare and Contrast** Write *U*, *S*, and *R* where urban, suburban, and rural environments are shown.

MALL

STOP

Changing the Environment

Oil rig

People change the environment to get natural resources. **Natural resources** are things from nature that we use. People drill for oil because oil helps make cars, trains, and buses go.

When people take away resources there can be negative, or bad, effects. Drilling for oil can hurt the air we breathe. Taking away resources can also change and destroy animals' habitats.

Sometimes there are drilling accidents. People drill for oil in the ocean using something called an oil rig. Sometimes oil spills out into the ocean, hurting fish and other animals.

Bird covered with oil

2. **Identify** one way people have changed the environment to get natural resources. **Write** the effect it has on the environment.

_____

_____

_____

_____

_____

People can take fewer resources from the environment. They can use less oil. People can walk or ride bicycles instead of driving cars.

People can change their environment to make it better. They dig paths in the soil to bring water to crops. They plant trees to replace ones that have been cut down. They take fewer fish from the water. This lets the number of fish grow. When they plant trees or protect fish, they are replenishing, or replacing, natural resources. This helps the habitat stay healthy.

If there is an oil spill, people can help clean up the water, plants, and animals. This is a positive, or good, way that people can change the environment.

Children planting a tree

3. **Identify** two ways people can replenish natural resources.

_____

_____

_____

_____

_____

_____

_____

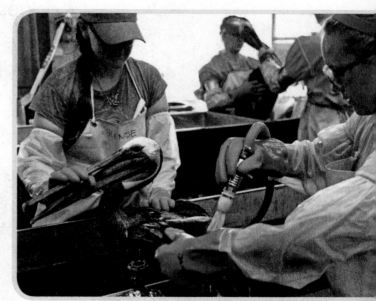

People washing oil off a bird

People Change the Water

One way people change Earth's water is by building dams. A dam is a wall across a river or stream. Dams hold water and help capture energy. People also change the water by building canals. A canal is a waterway that connects two bodies of water. Canals help people travel and move goods.

4. **Underline** two ways people change the water.

Making Life Easier

We change our environment to make life easier. These changes are important for how people work and live. Roads, bridges, and tunnels connect places so people can travel quickly from one place to another.

Hoover Dam

Pittsburgh, Pennsylvania

Farmers plow soil to plant seeds and grow crops. When there is not enough rain to grow crops, farmers irrigate their land. To irrigate means to move water to dry land. That makes it easier to grow more crops.

5. **Circle** the part of the picture that shows what irrigate means.

⬇ TEKS 7.C, 7.D, 8.A, 8.B, 8.C

6. **Cause and Effect** **Write** an effect that changing the environment can have.

_____

_____

7. **Is the environment where you live urban, suburban, or rural? Write one way you know.**   my **Story Ideas**

_____

_____

_____

8. **Write** one way that people change the environment to meet their needs.

_____

_____

_____

Where People Choose to Live

Envision It!

Look at the picture.

People make choices about where they will **settle,** or live. They think about how natural resources, the weather, and seasons affect what they want to do.

Natural Resources

When people pick a place to settle, they look for a place that has natural resources to meet their needs. Water is a resource that meets a need. People need forests for wood to build houses. They need land with good soil to grow food. Natural resources also affect the activities people can do. If a place is near water, people can swim, boat, or fish.

1. **Identify** three natural resources that affect where people settle.

_____

_____

_____

_____

Tell a partner what activities you might like to do in this environment.

Weather and Seasons

People may choose to live in a place where the weather is mostly warm so they can grow food year round. In a place that is mostly cold, people wear warm clothes and build houses that keep out the cold. Seasons affect the activities you can do and where you choose to live. You can swim outside in the summer and ski in the winter.

Natural hazards, or extreme weather, can affect where people settle. Earthquakes, tornadoes, and hurricanes are **natural hazards.** They can cause damage. People cannot do activities outside when there is extreme weather because it is dangerous.

2. ⊙ **Cause and Effect** <u>Underline</u> how the weather affects the activities people do and where they live.

Hurricane

PEARSON realize™   Go online to access your interactive digital lesson.

123

Types of Communities

You have learned about types of communities. The activities you like to do affect what type of community you choose to live in.

If you like to live close to many people, you may choose to live in an urban area. You may want to live near museums and theaters. You may want to go to restaurants. In an urban area, you can do these activities.

If you want to live in a community with open space, you might choose to live in the country. There are fewer people in a rural community. There is land to farm. You can ride horses and hike for miles. You may want to live somewhere in between like a suburb. In a suburb there are many people and activities, but there is also open space.

3. **Write** two things about each community that affect why people settle in it.

urban: _____

rural: _____

suburb: _____

Got it?

TEKS 7.A, 7.B

4. **Cause and Effect** How do natural resources affect where people live?

_____

_____

_____

_____

5. **Write** an activity that you like to do in the summer where you live.

my Story Ideas

_____

_____

6. How do natural hazards affect where people settle? Why?

_____

_____

_____

Cause and Effect

A cause is the reason something happens.
The effect is what happens.

Cause

Effect

Cause

Effect

Look at the picture of rain. The rain is a cause.
Follow the arrow. It points to a picture showing
an umbrella. Rainy weather caused the boy to
open his umbrella. That is the effect.

TEKS

SS 7.A Describe how weather patterns affect activities.
SS 19.B Create visual material such as graphic organizers to express ideas.
ELA 15.A Follow written multi-step directions.
ELA 15.B Use common graphic features to assist in the interpretation of text (e.g., illustrations).

Try it!

1. **Look** at the picture of people cleaning the beach. Are the people the cause or the effect?

   _____

   _____

   _____

2. **Write** the effect.

   _____

   _____

   _____

3. **Look** at the pictures below. **Draw** the missing effect and the missing cause in the empty boxes.

   Cause   **Effect**

   Cause   **Effect**

   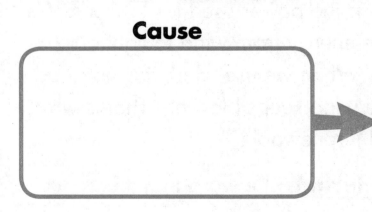

Earth's Resources

trees

wheat

Draw lines from the trees and the wheat to the product we make from them.

TEKS
7.B, 7.C, 8.C, 18.B

We get everything we need to live from nature. We get air to breathe and sunlight for energy. We even get oil to make gas for our cars. Nature is full of things for us to use. We call them natural resources.

Renewable Resources

A resource that can be replaced is called **renewable.** Water, wind, sunlight, and soil are all renewable resources. Natural processes can replace our water and soil. We will never run out of wind or sun.

Energy is the power used to do work. We can use energy from wind to light our homes. When we use wind, it is not used up. The wind keeps blowing. That is why we call it renewable.

1. **Underline** the word that means "can be replaced."

Wind turbines get energy from wind.

bread

pencil

UNLOCK THE BIG ?

I will know how to identify, use, and conserve resources.

Vocabulary

renewable

nonrenewable

conserve

Nonrenewable Resources

A resource that cannot be replaced is called **nonrenewable.** Oil and coal are two nonrenewable resources. We can burn coal to light our homes. When we burn coal, it is gone forever.

This pie chart shows how people in the United States use energy. A pie chart compares the amount of one thing to the amount of another. Use the pie chart to answer the question.

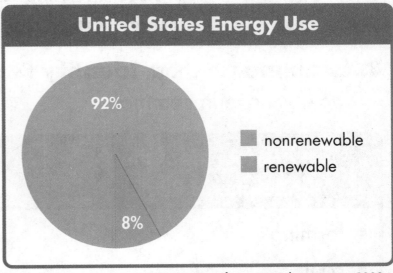

United States Energy Use

92%

8%

■ nonrenewable
■ renewable

Source: U.S. Energy Information Administration, 2009

2. ◉ **Draw Conclusions Fill in** the blank.

In the United States, we get most of our energy

_____

from _____ resources.

Regions and Resources

Different regions have different resources. Natural resources often affect where people choose to live. They affect how people live and work. The chart below lists the main resources in the Southeast and the Midwest. In the Southeast, much of the land is used for farming. People there may grow crops or raise animals on farms. People who live near the coasts may fish for their jobs. Other resources include coal, natural gas, and oil. In the Midwest, farming is an important resource. Thanks to the Midwest, the United States is one of the world's leading producers of farm products. Mining for coal and manufacturing are also important resources in this region.

3. **Examine** the chart. **Identify** two resources that the two regions have in common.

Resources of the Southeast Region	Resources of the Midwest Region
• farming • coal • fish/shellfish • hydroelectric power • natural gas • oil	• farming • livestock • dairy • coal • manufacturing

We Conserve Resources

Natural resources are important for our future. We need to **conserve,** or protect, the resources we use. Turn off the faucet to reduce the amount of water you use when you brush your teeth. Reuse plastic bags. Recycle paper, cans, plastic, and glass so they can be made into new things.

4. **Underline** two ways you can conserve resources.

 **Got it?**

TEKS 7.B, 7.C, 8.C

5. ◉ **Cause and Effect** Why do we conserve resources?

_____

_____

6. **Write** one natural resource that you use each day. How do you use it?

 **my Story Ideas**

_____

_____

_____

_____

7. **Write** one example of how natural resources affect where people live.

_____

_____

_____

_____

PEARSON realize Go online to access your interactive digital lesson.

131

Moving Ideas, People, and Things

These pictures show two ways that people can share their thoughts and ideas.

TEKS
5.A, 7.C, 8.A, 8.C

People, ideas, and goods move around the world every day. Technology makes these movements easier every year. **Technology** is the use of skills and tools.

Moving Ideas

Communication is the way people share ideas, thoughts, or information with each other. Today's technology makes communication fast and easy. You can use a computer to send letters, play games, learn, hear music, and watch movies. You can make a phone call from almost anywhere with a cell phone. A GPS, or global positioning system, is a way to tell someone your exact location anywhere in the world.

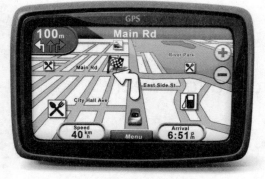

Global positioning system

1. ◉ **Cause and Effect** <u>Underline</u> one effect of new technology.

Draw a picture that shows a way to move people or goods.

UNLOCK THE BIG ?

I will know ways that people, things, and ideas are moved.

Vocabulary

technology
communication
transportation

Moving People

Transportation is a way to move people and goods. We travel on buses, in taxis, on subways, and in cars. When we travel in cars, we use roads and highways. Road maps or a GPS helps us get from one place to another.

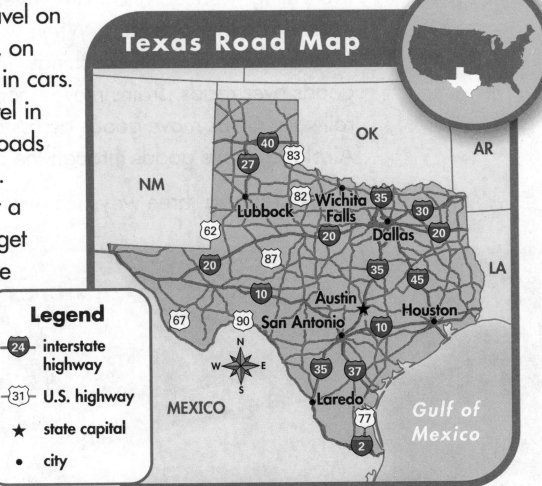

Texas Road Map

OK

NM

AR

Lubbock

Wichita Falls

Dallas

LA

Austin

Houston

San Antonio

MEXICO

Laredo

Gulf of Mexico

Legend

24 — interstate highway

31 — U.S. highway

★ state capital

• city

2. Circle Interstate 35 from Laredo to Austin.

Moving Things

Have you ever received a letter or a gift in the mail? How do you get groceries home from the store? Every day, people move big and small things from one place to another.

We make changes to the earth to make it easier to move things. We build roads. We blast tunnels through hills and mountains. We build bridges over rivers.

The United States cannot make or grow everything we need and want. Instead, we must trade with other countries. When we trade, we use transportation to move things. Trucks move goods over roads. Trains move goods across railways. Ships move goods across oceans. Airplanes move goods through the air.

3. Underline three ways we move things.

Helping One Another

We use communication and transportation to help people all over the world. When people need food or medicine, we can send help quickly. Helicopters send supplies to places that are hard to reach.

4. **Underline** two goods we can give to help people in need.

TEKS 7.C, 8.A

5. ◉ **Cause and Effect Write** a form of technology that has made communication or transportation easier.

_____

_____

6. ? How have you used transportation or communication today?

_____

_____

7. How have people changed the environment to meet a need?

_____

_____

_____

_____

Lesson 1   TEKS 6.B

1. **Circle** the absolute location.

The front of the class   On the desk   14 Main Street

Lesson 2 TEKS 5.B

2. **Draw** a simple map of an area in your community. Include a compass rose.

Lesson 3 TEKS 5.A

3. **Draw** a line from each word to its location on the globe.

equator

prime meridian

latitude

longitude

TEKS 6.A

Lesson 4

4. Draw and **label** two kinds of landforms.

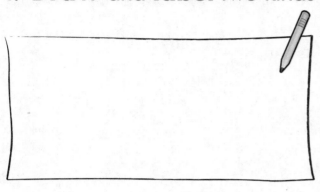
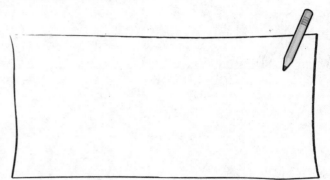

TEKS 7.A

Lesson 5

5. **Cause and Effect Complete** the sentence. **Circle** the best choice.

Amelia wears a warm coat and hat when the weather is

A warm and sunny.   **C** hot and wet.

B cold and windy.   **D** hot and dry.

TEKS 8.A

Lesson 6

6. Write two ways that people change their environment.

Lesson 7 🐾 TEKS 7.B

7. **Write** two ways that natural hazards affect people's lives.

Lesson 8 🐾 TEKS 8.C

8. **List** four items you can recycle to conserve natural resources.

Lesson 9 🐾 TEKS 7.C

9. **Write** how two types of transportation help us.

Go online to write and illustrate your own **myStory Book** using the **myStory Ideas** from this chapter.

What is the world like?

In this chapter you have learned about Earth and the plants, animals, and people who live here.

How do you think the world will be different 100 years from now? **Draw** a picture showing your predictions. Add a caption.

TEKS

SS 18.E
ELA 17

PEARSON
realize   Go online to access your interactive digital lesson.

139

Celebrating Our Traditions

my Story Spark

THE BIG ? **How is culture shared?**

my Story Video **Think** about stories your family tells. **Draw** a picture of how you celebrate your culture.

Texas Essential Knowledge and Skills

1.A Explain the significance of various community, state, and national celebrations such as Veterans Day, Memorial Day, Independence Day, and Thanksgiving.

4.A Identify contributions of historical figures, including Thurgood Marshall, Irma Rangel, John Hancock, and Theodore Roosevelt, who have influenced the community, state, and nation.

6.C Examine information from various sources about places and regions.

13.B Identify historical figures such as Paul Revere, Abigail Adams, World War II Women Airforce Service Pilots (WASPs) and Navajo Code Talkers, and Sojourner Truth who have exemplified good citizenship.

14.D Identify how selected customs, symbols, and celebrations reflect an American love of individualism, inventiveness, and freedom.

15.A Identify selected stories, poems, statues, paintings, and other examples of the local cultural heritage.

15.B Explain the significance of selected stories, poems, statues, paintings, and other examples of the local cultural heritage.

16.A Identify the significance of various ethnic and/or cultural celebrations.

16.B Compare ethnic and/or cultural celebrations.

18.A Obtain information about a topic using a variety of valid oral sources such as conversations, interviews, and music.

18.B Obtain information about a topic using a variety of valid visual sources such as pictures, maps, electronic sources, literature, reference sources, and artifacts.

18.E Interpret oral, visual, and print material by identifying the main idea, predicting, and comparing and contrasting.

19.A Express ideas orally based on knowledge and experiences.

19.B Create written and visual material such as stories, poems, maps, and graphic organizers to express ideas.

Begin With a Song

Festival Time

Sing to the tune of "Do Your Ears Hang Low?"

There's a festival,

Please come along with me.

We'll attend a ceremony,

There's a lot to do and see.

We can learn about our culture.

What a fun time it will be,

At the festival.

PEARSON realize   Go online to access your interactive digital lesson.

141

Vocabulary Preview

culture

language

tradition

artifact

festival

Identify examples of these words and (circle) them in the picture.

CULTURE FESTIVAL

custom

holiday

hero

veteran

landmark

Culture Is Our Way of Life

Different families eat different foods.

TEKS
13.B, 15.A, 15.B, 18.A, 18.B

Culture is a way of life. Culture includes our family, friends, and our community. It includes the foods we eat, the clothing we wear, and the places we live. Language, music, and religion are part of culture, too. It is the heritage that people pass down to their children.

Our Language

Bonjour! (bohn ZHOR) This is what children in France say when they greet a friend. It means "hello." People all around the world have different ways of saying the same thing. **Language** uses spoken and written words to communicate ideas and feelings. Greetings are part of every culture.

Aloha

Ciao

Hola

Jambo!

Yiasou

Every language has its own way to say hello.

1. ◉ **Main Idea and Details** <u>Underline</u> one way we greet each other in American culture.

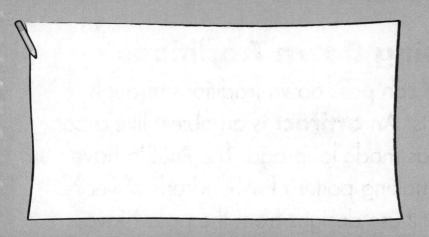

Draw a food that you like to eat.

Vocabulary

culture   tradition
language   artifact

Our Music

Music can make us feel happy. Music is an important part of every culture. It is something people both young and old can enjoy. We hum, sing, clap our hands, and dance.

Every culture makes its own music. Different kinds of instruments are used to produce special sounds.

Many children learn how to play instruments from their parents or grandparents. When children grow up, they teach their own children how to play their culture's music. This is called a tradition. A **tradition** is something that is passed down over time.

2. Work with a partner to identify songs from your local culture and tell why they are important.

Calypso is a kind of music played on drums, rattles, and guitars in the West Indies.

Pueblo pot

Passing Down Traditions

People can pass down traditions through artifacts. An **artifact** is an object like a pot that was made long ago. The Pueblo have been making pottery for hundreds of years. They still use designs from the past. Navajo (nah vah HOH) children learn to weave from watching and talking to their parents and grandparents. The traditions that are passed down to us through our families make up our cultural heritage.

3. **Circle** how Navajo children learn to weave.

Navajo Code Talkers

Language is a tradition that can be passed down, too. The Navajo language is very old. It was used to help the United States in World War II. Young Navajo men wanted to honor their country. They used their language to make a code.

Navajo Code Talkers send a message.

Navajo soldiers sent radio messages in the code.
No one else could understand what the messages
said. The Navajo Code Talkers helped to win the war.

4. **Write** how Navajo Code Talkers honored their country.

_____

_____

_____

Got it?

TEKS 15.A, 15.B, 18.A, 18.B

5. **Compare and Contrast** How is one culture you have read about like your culture?

_____

_____

_____

_____

6. **What is a tradition that you share with your family?**

my Story Ideas

_____

_____

_____

7. **Talk** to a family member, such as a parent or grandparent, about your cultural heritage. **Ask** if your family has any artifacts, or things that have been passed down. **Write** down what you learn.

Cultures in Our Country

Envision It!

Families in the United States celebrate Thanksgiving.

TEKS
1.A, 14.D, 16.A, 16.B, 18.E

People from all over the world come to the United States to live. They bring their culture, heritage, and customs. A **custom** is a special way a group does something.

San Antonio, Texas

Long ago, France tried to occupy part of Mexico. On May 5, 1862, a small Mexican army fought a big French army at Puebla. The Mexican army won.

Every year, people in San Antonio have a **festival** to celebrate freedom and the bravery of the Mexican army. It is called Cinco de Mayo, or the Fifth of May. One custom is for Mariachi (mahr ee AH chee) bands to play while dancers perform.

1. **Underline** a custom you might see at a Cinco de Mayo celebration.

People wear colorful costumes on Cinco de Mayo.

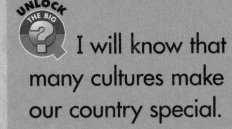

UNLOCK THE BIG ? I will know that many cultures make our country special.

Vocabulary

festival

custom

Write what this photograph tells you about the United States.

New Orleans, Louisiana

Long ago, people from different cultures settled in New Orleans. They brought music from Africa, France, Spain, Ireland, and Germany. Their music mixed to become the American music called jazz. Jazz musicians have a custom. Each individual musician in a band takes a turn making up new music as the band plays.

Jazz is a big part of community life in New Orleans. It is played at baseball games, dances, and funerals. Every spring, people visit New Orleans to attend Mardi Gras. Like mariachi bands do for Cinco de Mayo, jazz musicians march down the streets at Mardi Gras while people clap and cheer!

2. **⊙ Main Idea and Details**
   Underline how jazz shows individualism.

Jazz musicians march in a Mardi Gras parade in New Orleans.

San Francisco, California

Many Chinese Americans in San Francisco live in Chinatown. In this neighborhood, children speak both English and Chinese. They also celebrate the Chinese New Year.

An American New Year is always on January 1. A Chinese New Year can be in January or February. A big Chinese New Year parade is a custom that blends American culture with Chinese culture. A special dragon is carried down the street by more than 100 people! The people invent ways to make the dragon jump and slither like a snake. It rises, shakes, and dives at the crowd. This celebration is a way that Americans show their love of inventiveness, or creating new things.

Chinese New Year parade

150

An American custom that many cultures celebrate is Thanksgiving. People spend this national holiday with their families and friends. They remember early settlers in our country who were thankful for their first harvest.

Thanksgiving Day parade

3. **Underline** a custom that many American cultures enjoy.

TEKS 14.D, 16.A, 16.B, 18.E

4. **Compare and Contrast** How are the cultures of San Francisco and New Orleans alike and different?

_____

_____

_____

_____

_____

_____

5. What is a cultural celebration or custom that your community shares?    my Story Ideas

_____

_____

6. **Write** one inventive way Americans can make a custom or celebration their own.

_____

_____

Compare and Contrast

We compare to find out how two things are alike. We contrast to find out how they are different. Look at the paragraphs and pictures about soccer and rugby. Details that show how they are alike are underlined. Details that show how they are different are circled.

Many children in the United States play soccer. Soccer is a sport that is played by kicking a ball and moving it. Soccer players run a lot. Players kick the ball into the goal to score a point.

Many children in New Zealand play rugby. Rugby is a sport that is played by holding a ball and moving it. Rugby players run a lot. When players get to the end of the field, they score points.

 **Try it!**

Read the paragraphs aloud with a partner. Then compare and contrast your ideas on what you hear about cricket and baseball.

> Cricket is a sport played with a bat and a ball. Each team has eleven players on it. A game can last for several days.
>
> Baseball is a sport played with a bat and a ball. Each team has nine players on it. Some baseball games can last four hours.

1. **Write** one way that cricket and baseball are alike.

_____

_____

_____

2. **Write** one way that cricket and baseball are different.

_____

_____

_____

PEARSON **realize** | Go online to access your interactive digital lesson.

153

Texas

Lesson 3

What We Celebrate

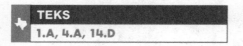

July

SUN	MON	TUE	WED	THU	FRI	SAT
					1	2
3	4	5	6	7	8	9
10	11	12	13	14	15	16
17	18	19	20	21	22	23
24	25	26	27	28	29	30
31						

Look at the month of July.

TEKS
1.A, 4.A, 14.D

Americans celebrate
Independence Day.

A **holiday** is a special day. On national holidays, we celebrate important people and events from our country's past.

A Nation Is Born

Long ago, people in our country lived in 13 colonies. A **colony** is a place that is ruled by a country far away. England ruled the American colonies. People in the colonies did not think England's laws were fair. They fought a war against England and won their freedom.

Every year we celebrate our country's freedom on Independence Day. We have parades and picnics. We watch fireworks. We wave flags as a symbol of our country's birthday and our love of freedom.

1. **Underline** what we celebrate on Independence Day.

Name a special day when we watch fireworks.

Remembering Our Heroes

A **hero** is someone who is remembered for bravery or good deeds. Our country has two national holidays to honor special heroes who protect our country. People march in parades and give speeches.

On Memorial Day, we remember United States citizens who died in war. Memorial Day is celebrated on the last Monday in May.

A **veteran** is someone who has served in the armed forces. Each November, Veterans Day honors the people who fought to keep our country free.

2. **Underline** the two holidays that honor special heroes in our country.

We honor veterans each November.

PEARSON **realize** · · · Go online to access your interactive digital lesson.

155

Thomas Jefferson

Remembering Government Leaders

Thomas Jefferson was the third president of the United States. Before he became the president, he wrote the Declaration of Independence. President Theodore Roosevelt treated workers fairly and supported conservation. He also won a prize for helping to end a war. On Presidents' Day in February, we celebrate them as individuals who thought of inventive new ways to help our country.

3. **Write** the name of another president.

_____

- - - - - - - - - - - - - - - - - - -

Remembering Community Leaders

For a long time, African Americans were not treated fairly in the United States because of the color of their skin.

Dr. Martin Luther King, Jr. believed that all Americans should be treated equally. Dr. King spoke out against unfair laws and helped to pass new ones.

Theodore Roosevelt

Dr. King gave a famous speech in 1963. He shared his dream that one day all people would respect one another. We honor Dr. King and celebrate his birthday every January.

Dr. Martin Luther King, Jr.

4.  **Main Idea and Details**
   <u>Underline</u> one reason we honor Dr. Martin Luther King, Jr.

Got it?

TEKS 1.A, 4.A, 14.D

5. **Compare and Contrast** How are Memorial Day and Veterans Day alike? How are they different?

_____

_____

_____

_____

6. **THE BIG ?** How do you and your family celebrate holidays in your community?

my Story Ideas

_____

_____

7. On a separate sheet of paper, **write** two ways Theodore Roosevelt helped our nation.

American Stories

Johnny has
many seeds.

Johnny plants
an apple seed.

TEKS
15.A, 15.B, 18.B, 18.E, 19.B

American stories are an important part of
our cultural heritage. Some stories have
facts, or parts that are true. Some have
parts that are **fiction,** or make-believe.

Folk Tales

A **folk tale** is a story from long ago
about the lives of real people. Read these
folk tales about three famous Americans.

Davy Crockett

Davy Crockett was born in a cabin
in Tennessee in 1786. As a boy, he worked
hard to buy a horse and became a great
bear hunter. Davy was a soldier who fought
at the Battle of the Alamo in Texas. He was a
government leader, too.

1.  **Main Idea and Details**
   Underline one fact about Davy Crockett.

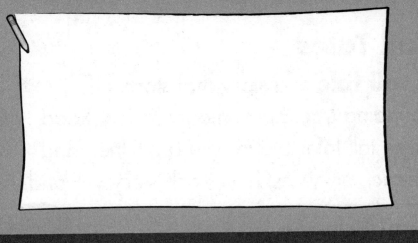

Draw what you think will happen next.

Vocabulary

facts   folk tale

fiction   tall tale

Johnny Appleseed

Johnny Appleseed got his name because he carried sacks of apple seeds everywhere he went. His real name was John Chapman. Johnny planted many apple trees across the country. He wanted people to have enough food to eat.

2. **Underline** Johnny Appleseed's real name.

Betsy Ross

Betsy Ross made her living by sewing. One day in 1776, General George Washington, the leader of the American army, visited her. He asked Betsy to sew the first American flag. Betsy made a flag with 13 stars and stripes, one for each American colony.

3. **Underline** how Betsy Ross made her living.

Tall Tales

A **tall tale** is a story that starts off sounding true, but is mostly fiction. Read these tall tales aloud with a partner, and predict, or guess, how each story will end.

Paul Bunyan

When Paul Bunyan was a baby, he was so big that he ate 40 bowls of oatmeal each day! Paul had a giant blue ox named Babe. He and Babe stomped around Minnesota as they played. Their footprints were huge. The holes filled up with rain and made 10,000 lakes!

Pecos Bill

Stories say that Pecos Bill was the best cowboy to ever live. He had a horse that no one else could ride. One day, there was a tornado. Pecos Bill jumped on it. The tornado flattened forests. It rained so hard that the canyons washed away. He did not let go until the tornado died down to nothing. That is how cowboys got the idea to ride horses in rodeos.

4. **Underline** part of each story that is fiction.

John Henry

There have been songs and books written about a railroad worker named John Henry. Some say that he was bigger and taller than any other man around. John Henry used his hammer to chip away at rock so that a big tunnel could be built. With a hammer in each hand, John Henry built the tunnel all by himself!

5. **Underline** part of the story that is fiction.

Got it?

TEKS 15.A, 15.B, 18.B, 18.E, 19.B

6. ◉ **Compare and Contrast** How are folk tales and tall tales alike? How are they different?

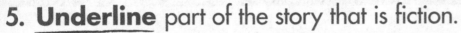

_____

_____

_____

7. ❓ Why are American tales important?

 my Story Ideas

_____

_____

_____

8. On a separate sheet of paper, **write** your own tall tale. Read aloud the first part of your story to a partner. Have your partner **interpret** the story by **predicting** how it will end. Then read the rest of the story. **Talk** about what you wrote.

Two Cultures

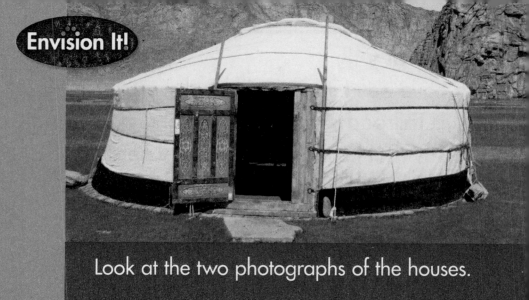

Look at the two photographs of the houses.

TEKS
6.C, 14.D, 15.A, 15.B, 18.E

Cultures around the world meet the needs of their people in different ways. Read about how the cultures in Mexico City and Beijing are alike and different.

Culture in Mexico City

Mexico City is the capital of Mexico. There are parks and museums to visit. You can shop or eat in the city's many neighborhoods. Along the streets, there are people selling tasty food like tacos and tamales. At night, traditional music and dances are performed in the city.

The most popular sport in Mexico City is soccer. Many children play it after school and on weekends. Look at the picture of the boys playing soccer. Think about what it tells you about culture in Mexico City.

UNLOCK
THE BIG
? I will know about
two different cultures.

Vocabulary

ruins
landmark

Circle one thing that is alike.
Put an **X** on one thing that is different.

A long time ago, a group of people called the Aztecs lived in Mexico. Today, visitors from around the world visit Aztec **ruins,** or buildings that were lived in long ago.

Look at the picture of the Mexican flag. An eagle, a snake, and a cactus on the flag are symbols that were used by the Aztecs long ago. The color green on the flag stands for independence and a love of freedom. Like the United States, Mexico fought to become free from another country.

PACIFIC
OCEAN

ATLANTIC
OCEAN

Mexico★
City

The Mexican flag and a map that shows the location of Mexico City, Mexico

1. **Underline** the symbols that are on the Mexican flag.

Aztec ruins in Mexico

PEARSON
realize   Go online to access your
interactive digital lesson.   163

The Chinese flag and a map that shows the location of Beijing, China

Culture in Beijing

Beijing is the capital of China. It is a city that blends old and new. Many skyscrapers, or tall buildings, stand next to buildings from long ago. Many people in Beijing ride bikes. Riding bikes is a popular form of transportation in the city.

Tiananmen Square is where celebrations and events have taken place for hundreds of years. Today, people fly kites. People do tai chi, a slow exercise that helps people stay relaxed and healthy. People also stop to eat food that is sold in the square, like noodles, dumplings, and seafood.

Look at the picture of China's flag. The big star is a symbol of China. The small stars are symbols of the people of China.

Many people in Beijing ride bikes to get around.

Many visitors come to see the Great Wall of China. This **landmark,** or a structure that is important to a particular place, is more than 2,000 years old and thousands of miles long.

2.  **Main Idea and Details** <u>**Underline**</u> three things you can do if you visit Beijing.

Got it?

⬇ TEKS 6.C, 14.D, 18.E

3. **Compare and Contrast** How are Mexico City and Beijing alike? How are they different?

_____

_____

_____

_____

4. **?** THE BIG How is American culture like other cultures? **my Story Ideas**

_____

_____

_____

_____

5. On a separate sheet of paper, **write** how the Mexican flag shows what Mexico and the United States have in common.

Using Graphic Sources

A chart tells information in columns and rows. Columns run up and down. Rows run left and right.

Countries and Cultures			
Country	Greeting	Landmark	Food
China	Ni hao		
Mexico	Hola		
United States			

TEKS

SS 18.B Obtain information about a topic using visual sources.
SS 19.B Create visual material such as graphic organizers to express ideas.
ELA 25.C Record basic information in simple visual formats (e.g., charts, picture graphs).

This chart is about cultures in different countries. The columns tell what information you will learn. The rows tell what countries the information is about.

1. Which three countries are named on the chart?

2. **Circle** a landmark found in China.

3. How do you greet someone in Chinese?

4. **Draw** a square around a food eaten in Mexico.

5. **Complete** the last row of the chart. **Write** or **draw** information about the United States in each column.

6. You want to add the capital of each country to this chart. Would you add a new row or a new column?

Lesson 1 TEKS 18.B

1. **Circle** the photograph that shows an artifact.

Lesson 2 TEKS 16.B, 18.E

2. **Compare and Contrast Look** at the photographs. **Write** how these cultural celebrations are alike and different.

Alike:

Different:

Lesson 3   🔸 **TEKS 1.A**

3. Draw a line to match each holiday with what we celebrate.

Independence Day   respect for all people

Veterans Day   heroes who protect
                                    our country

Dr. Martin Luther King, Jr. Day   our country's freedom

Lesson 4   🔸 **TEKS 18.E, 19.B**

4. Draw a picture of your favorite folk or tall tale. **Write** one
   reason you like it.

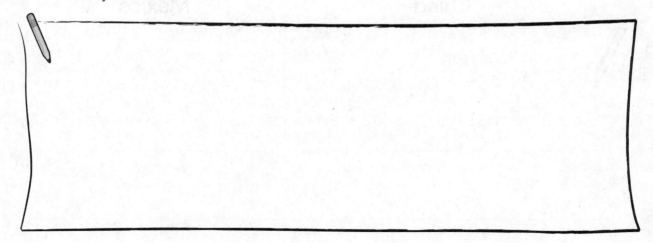

Lesson 5  TEKS 15.A, 18.E

5. Complete the sentence. **Circle** the best answer.

A food that is part of the Mexican culture is

A pizza   **C** hot dogs

B dumplings   **D** tamales

6. Write what the photographs below tell you about culture in China and Mexico.

China

Mexico

Go online to write and illustrate your own **myStory Book** using the **myStory Ideas** from this chapter.

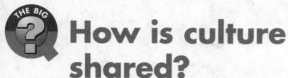 **How is culture shared?**

TEKS

SS 1.A, 16.A, 16.B, 18.A, 19.A, 19.B

ELA 17

In this chapter, you have learned about cultures in different parts of the world.

Think about your own culture. **Talk** to a friend or family member about celebrations in your culture.
Talk about one thing you know about your culture.
Talk about one custom you have experienced.

Draw a picture of a custom in your culture. **Write** a caption. Share your picture. **Tell** a partner about it.

Our Nation Past and Present

How does life change throughout history?

Draw a picture of something in your community or family that has changed over time.

★ Texas Essential Knowledge and Skills

1.A Explain the significance of various community, state, and national celebrations such as Veterans Day, Memorial Day, Independence Day, and Thanksgiving.

1.B Identify and explain the significance of various community, state, and national landmarks such as monuments and government buildings.

2.A Describe the order of events by using designations of time periods such as historical and present times.

2.B Apply vocabulary related to chronology, including past, present, and future.

2.C Create and interpret timelines for events in the past and present.

3.A Identify several sources of information about a given period or event such as reference materials, biographies, newspapers, and electronic sources.

3.B Describe various evidence of the same time period using primary sources such as photographs, journals, and interviews.

4.A Identify contributions of historical figures, including Thurgood Marshall, Irma Rangel, John Hancock, and Theodore Roosevelt, who have influenced the community, state, and nation.

4.B Identify historical figures such as Amelia Earhart, W. E. B. DuBois, Robert Fulton, and George Washington Carver who have exhibited individualism and inventiveness.

4.C Explain how people and events have influenced local community history.

5.A Interpret information on maps and globes using basic map elements such as title, orientation (north, south, east, west), and legend/map keys.

7.C Explain how people depend on the physical environment and natural resources to meet basic needs.

7.D Identify the characteristics of different communities, including urban, suburban, and rural, and how they affect activities and settlement patterns.

13.B Identify historical figures such as Paul Revere, Abigail Adams, World War II Women Airforce Service Pilots (WASPs) and Navajo Code Talkers, and Sojourner Truth who have exemplified good citizenship.

13.C Identify other individuals who exemplify good citizenship.

15.A Identify selected stories, poems, statues, paintings, and other examples of the local cultural heritage.

15.B Explain the significance of selected stories, poems, statues, paintings, and other examples of the local cultural heritage.

17.A Describe how science and technology change communication, transportation, and recreation.

17.B Explain how science and technology change the ways in which people meet basic needs.

18.A Obtain information about a topic using a variety of valid oral sources such as conversations, interviews, and music.

18.B Obtain information about a topic using a variety of valid visual sources such as pictures, maps, electronic sources, literature, reference sources, and artifacts.

18.C Use various parts of a source, including the table of contents, glossary, and index, as well as keyword Internet searches to locate information.

18.D Sequence and categorize information.

19.B Create written and visual material such as stories, poems, maps, and graphic organizers to express ideas.

 # Begin With a Song

Living in America

by Henry Delaney

Sing to the tune of "Skip to My Lou."

Long ago they sailed the sea,
Traveled far with family.
Built homes in each colony,
They came to America.

Soon they wanted to be free,
Living independently.
Fighting for their liberty,
Living in America.

Vocabulary Preview

history

monument

explorer

settler

immigrant

Identify examples of these words and (circle) them in the picture.

pioneer

ancient

invention

civil rights

innovator

Life Then and Now

Look at the pictures above.

TEKS
1.B, 2.A, 2.B, 4.C, 7.C, 7.D, 15.A

History is the story of the past. It tells about events that happened long ago. Each community and family has its own history. Each person has a history, too.

You Then and Now

What were you like in the past? You were very small when you were born. Over time, you grew and learned to walk and talk. When we talk about the past, we use the words *yesterday* and *then*.

What can you do today? You are in school, and you can read and write. When we talk about the present, we use the words *today* and *now*. *Tomorrow* tells about the future.

1. **Circle** words that tell about the past. **Underline** words that tell about the present. **Draw** a box around words that tell about the future.

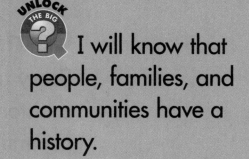

I will know that people, families, and communities have a history.

Vocabulary

history   century

generation   monument

Families Then and Now

Events that happened in your family's past are your family history. You can ask a parent or guardian what life was like when they were your age. A family member from a different **generation,** or age group, can tell you how life has changed or stayed the same over time.

Long ago, families needed clothing, food, and a home. Today your family needs these things, too. However, there are differences between life then and now. Many families once grew their food in gardens. Today, most families buy food at the market. Families long ago played games, but they did not play them on a computer.

2. **Underline** two things that have changed in family life over time.

Communities Then and Now

Every person has a history. Every place has a history, too. People who have lived in your community for many years can tell about its history. Most communities begin with a small group called founders. When more people move to the community, the community grows. It may change from rural to urban. More homes, schools, stores, and roads may be built.

Communities Change

Sometimes a problem can cause a community to change. That happened to the people in the community of Enterprise, Alabama. About a **century,** or 100 years, ago, Enterprise was a rural community that grew a lot of cotton. Then, a bug called a boll weevil destroyed most of the cotton. The farmers knew they needed to grow something that the boll weevil would not eat.

Many farmers in the South had cotton crops that were destroyed by the boll weevil.

They discovered that peanuts grew well and the boll weevil did not eat peanuts. Today, many farmers in Enterprise still grow peanuts. The people in Enterprise built a monument in their community. A **monument** is a statue that honors a person or event. Solving the boll weevil problem was a big event in Enterprise's history!

3. ⊙ **Draw Conclusions** <u>Underline</u> one reason people in Enterprise built a monument.

TEKS 2.B

4. ⊙ **Fact and Opinion** **Write** one fact about a person who is part of your family history.

_____

_____

5. ⊙ How has your family or community changed from the past to the present?

my Story Ideas

_____

_____

_____

6. On a separate sheet of paper, **write** a list of three ways that you have changed from the past to the present.

Reading and Creating a Timeline

A timeline shows the order in which events happened. You read a timeline from left to right, just like a sentence. Look at the timeline of Austin, Texas. It shows some important events that happened there in the past and present.

You can create a timeline of events in the past and present of your own life. Draw a line from left to right. Add each year since you were born. Then you can mark a spot that shows when important events happened. You might mark when you were born, when you started school, and an event from this year.

Austin's Community Timeline

1920	1940	1960

1935
Almost 20 inches of rain caused the Colorado River to flood downtown Austin.

1961
Many new schools were built as Austin's population grew 40 percent in the early 1960s.

Learning Objective

I will know how to read a timeline.

TEKS

SS 2.A Describe the order of events by using designations of time periods.

SS 2.C Create and interpret timelines for events in the past and present.

ELA 25.C Record basic information in simple visual formats.

Try it!

1. What does this timeline show?

_____

- -

_____

2. **Circle** the event in the present that is more than 25 years old.

3. **Create** a timeline of historical, or past, and present events in your life.

| 1980 | 2000 | 2020 |

2000
Austin citizens celebrated the 2000 presidential election at the Texas State Capitol.

2013
The South by Southwest® Festival celebrates 26 years.

PEARSON realize™ Go online to access your interactive digital lesson.

181

Texas

Lesson 2

Learning About the Past

Look at the photographs. They show the Alamo in San Antonio, Texas, long ago and today.

TEKS
3.A, 3.B, 18.A, 18.B, 18.C

You can learn about the past by talking to people, reading books, and looking at objects. All of these are sources for learning about life long ago.

Primary Sources

A primary source is something that helps you learn about people, places, and events from the past. A **primary source** is a material that was written or made by someone who saw an event happen. Photographs, paintings, and drawings are some primary sources. They show what people looked like and what they wore in the past.

Journals, letters, and maps are also primary sources. A **journal,** or diary, is a daily record of thoughts and events in a person's life.

This journal tells about a journey across the United States in 1805.

UNLOCK THE BIG ?

I will know the difference between primary and secondary sources.

Vocabulary

primary source
journal
secondary source
biography

rcle something that is the same in both pictures.
ark an X on something that changed.

Secondary Sources

A secondary source also helps you learn about the past. However, a **secondary source** is written or made by someone who did not see an event happen. A **biography,** or book about another person's life, is a secondary source. This textbook is a secondary source, too!

People who study and write about history are called historians. Historians use many primary and secondary sources to learn and write about people and events of long ago. Each reference source gives clues about a person's life or an event that took place in the past.

1. ⊙ **Main Idea and Details**
   Underline three sources you can use to learn about the past.

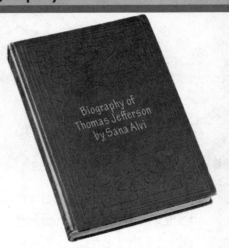

A biography is a secondary source.

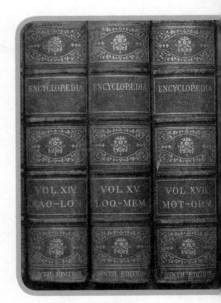

Encyclopedias are secondary sources.

PEARSON realize. Go online to access your interactive digital lesson.

183

Using Sources

The library in your school or community has primary and secondary sources. Some of these are reference materials like books, maps, newspapers, magazines, and encyclopedias. You might also find music and songs. Many songs tell stories about events and people in the past. Museums contain sources called artifacts. An artifact is an object, like a coin or a stamp, that was made or used by people long ago.

Libraries or museums may have primary sources for local history. One source may be interviews with people who lived long ago in your community. You can listen to, watch, or read these interviews. Your own family is a primary source for history, too. You can interview family members about when they were growing up. There may be photographs that show family events. They may also have a journal written by a relative. The journal may tell about life long ago.

2. **Interview** a family member and have a conversation with another family member to learn about your family history.

A library is a good place to look for information about the past.

Using Electronic Sources

You can also learn about history by using your computer and the Internet. If you type in key words about a topic, you will discover many Web sites about that topic. Many libraries and museums have their own Web sites where you can search for sources to learn about history.

There are tools to help you learn about history on the Internet. A Web browser is a computer program that shows Web sites. A search engine is a Web site that lets you search for information about any topic you want. It is like a library catalog. Choose Web sites that are trustworthy. Government and state history sites are good sources. Check more than one site if you are not sure the information you find is correct.

3. **Write** some key words you would use to search for information about what children wore to school long ago.

_____

_____

_____

_____

Contents

BELL PEPPERS $1.49 lb. ONIONS $1.29 lb. TOMATOES $2.99 lb. ZUCCHINI $1.29 lb.

Index

advertisements 12
bulk price 11
checkout 14
comparison shopping 7
coupons 4, 14
displays 5
expiration date
  (sell-by date) 7, 13
generic (store-brand)
  products 12
individual price 8, 11
ingredients 7
layout 5–6
name-brand products 12
packaging 9, 11, 12
receipt 14

shelf sticker 8
signs 6
unit price 8–9
volume 7, 9, 10
  fluid ounce 10
  gallon 10
  liter 10
  milliliter 10
  pint 9, 10
  quart 10
weight 7, 9, 10
  gram 10
  kilogram 10
  ounce 9, 10
  pound 9, 10

answer to question on page 11: The 10-pack of paper towels is the better deal. You pay $1 per roll, or if you bought 10 si $2 each, you them (10

Glossary

bulk	a great size or amount
comparison	looking at what makes two or more things the same or different
consume	to use up
coupons	pieces of paper that can be used to save money on a store item
expiration	ending time; an expiration date is the date at which a product is no longer safe to use
generic	without a brand name
individual	single
items	separate things that are part of a group
layout	the way a space is laid out or arranged
receipt	a paper that lists purchases and th amount of money paid
volume	the amount of space insi has a length, a wid

Using Parts of a Source

Print books are also good sources for learning about history. An encyclopedia is a reference book that has topics in alphabetical order. Many books have special parts that help you find information easily. These parts are the table of contents, the index, and the glossary.

The table of contents is in the front of a book. It lists the titles of all the chapters in the book. Chapter titles often let you know what you will learn about in that chapter. The table of contents also lists the page number where each chapter begins.

The index is in the back of a book. It lists the topics in the book in alphabetical order and the page number where they can be found. It is useful when you want to find information about a specific topic, place, or person.

The glossary is also in the back. It gives the meaning of difficult words that were used in the book. Sometimes, it also tells how to say them.

4. **<u>Underline</u>** the parts of a print book that help you find information.

5. If you wanted to know the meaning of a word in a book, where would you look?

_____

_____

TEKS 3.A, 3.B, 18.A, 18.B

6. **◉ Fact and Opinion** Is this statement a fact or an opinion? _Primary sources are better than secondary sources._ Which word is the clue?

_____

_____

7. **THE BIG ?** **Write** one way you can learn about change over time by studying primary sources.

my **Story Ideas**

_____

_____

_____

8. **Write** a list of the different kinds of sources you could use to find information about something you want to learn about.

_____

_____

_____

The First Americans

A.

B.

Look at the photographs of the different shelters.

TEKS
4.C, 5.A, 7.C, 18.C

The first people to live in America were **American Indians.** Three American Indian groups, the Plains, Pueblo, and Timucua (tee moo KWAH), lived in different regions. Each group depended on natural resources from their environment to meet their needs for food, clothes, and shelter.

Plains people hunted buffalo for food, clothing, and shelter. They lived in teepees made of buffalo hides and wooden poles.

Pueblo people grew corn to eat and cotton for clothes. They hunted deer and antelope. Pueblo homes were made from clay bricks.

Timucua people hunted bear and deer for food and clothes. Farmers planted corn, beans, and squash. Timucua homes were made from palm trees.

Plains teepee

A. _____

B. _____

Write the material that was used to make each shelter.

Vocabulary

American Indians

1. ◎ **Main Idea and Details Look** at the map. **Write** "B" on the group that used buffalo for food, clothing, and shelter.

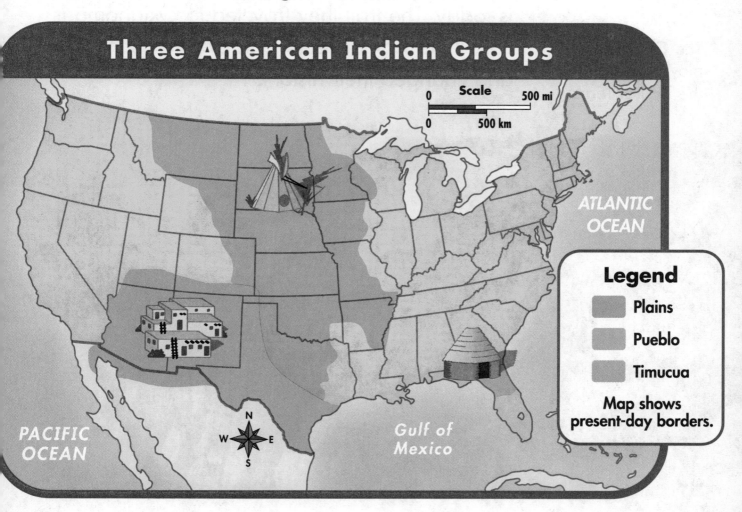

Three American Indian Groups

Scale
0 _____ 500 mi
0 _____ 500 km

ATLANTIC OCEAN

PACIFIC OCEAN

Gulf of Mexico

N W E S

Legend
- Plains
- Pueblo
- Timucua

Map shows present-day borders.

Cherokee History

Long ago, American Indians called the Cherokee lived where the states of Tennessee and Georgia are today. Their leader was called a chief. The Cherokee farmed corn, squash, beans, and sunflowers. They caught fish for food. They made some of their clothes from animal skins. They made their homes with branches and clay.

When people from Europe came to America, they fought the Cherokee for their land. They wanted to settle on it. The Cherokee were forced to move to an area where the state of Oklahoma is today. The trail they traveled to Oklahoma is called the Trail of Tears. This event influenced and changed their history.

The Cherokee moved west along the Trail of Tears.

Wilma Mankiller was the first woman chief of the Cherokee. She worked with teachers to make Cherokee schools in Oklahoma better. She made healthcare better for Cherokee people, too. In 1998, Wilma Mankiller received the Medal of Freedom from President Bill Clinton for her hard work.

2. **Underline** two things Wilma Mankiller did for her people and her local community.

 **Got it?**

🐾 TEKS 7.C, 18.C

3. ◉ **Fact and Opinion Write** a fact about how Pueblo people used natural resources to meet needs.

_____

_____

4. 🅠 **Write** one thing that changed for Cherokee people.

 my Story Ideas

_____

_____

5. Using books or an Internet keyword search, **find out** about an American Indian group from the region you live in. **Write** a list of three things you learn.

_____

_____

America's Early Settlers

Write a label for each picture. Tell how people long ago might have used the items.

TEKS
1.A, 4.A, 4.C, 13.B, 13.C

Long ago, explorers from Europe sailed to North America searching for gold and land. An **explorer** is a person who is the first to travel to a new place. **Settlers,** or people who make a home in a new land, followed the explorers.

Europeans in America

Spanish settlers built a colony in Florida called St. Augustine. A colony is a community ruled by a country far away. Shortly after, English settlers built the colony of Jamestown in Virginia. American Indians often lost land when colonies were built.

Vocabulary

explorer

settler

Pilgrim

Life was hard for the early settlers. They did not have much food, and winters were very cold.

Another English colony was called Plymouth. It was in what is now Massachusetts. Plymouth was settled by people called the **Pilgrims.** The Pilgrims came so they could practice their own religion. American Indians influenced the colony by helping them grow crops such as corn, squash, and beans. On Thanksgiving we remember a feast the Pilgrims and American Indians shared.

1. ◎ **Compare and Contrast Look** at the picture. Circle three ways life was different long ago.

Thirteen Colonies, One Country

Many colonists came to North America. In time, there were 13 English colonies. England made laws for the colonies and forced colonists to pay taxes. Many colonists grew unhappy. They wanted to be independent and make their own laws. Some colonists influenced others to act.

John and Abigail Adams were colonists who spoke out against England's rule. John Adams said that the colonies should declare their freedom. Thomas Jefferson wrote a document called the Declaration of Independence. It said the people in the colonies wanted to be free. John Hancock was the first person to sign the Declaration of Independence.

England did not want the colonies to be free. England and the colonies fought a long war called the American Revolution.

Members of Congress from each colony signed the Declaration of Independence.

George Washington and soldiers of the American Revolution

194

George Washington led the army for the American colonists. In the end, the colonists won their freedom. The colonies became states. George Washington became the first president of our new country, called the United States of America.

2. **Underline** how John Hancock showed he wanted the colonies to be free.

TEKS 1.A, 4.C

3. **Fact and Opinion** What was John Adams's opinion about England's rule?

_____

_____

_____

4. How was living in the colonies different from living in the United States today?

_____

_____

_____

_____

5. Why is Thanksgiving celebrated?

_____

_____

_____

_____

A Growing Nation

Envision It!

compass

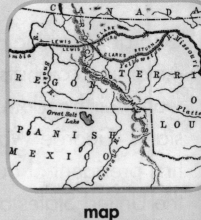

map

Look at the artifacts above.

TEKS
1.B, 4.B, 5.A, 7.D, 15.A, 15.B

As the United States grew, more and more immigrants came to live here. An **immigrant** is a person who moves from one country to another. The eastern United States was getting crowded. It was time to explore the West!

Moving West

Sacagawea

Meriwether Lewis and William Clark left St. Louis, Missouri in 1804 to explore and map the West. Sacagawea (sak uh juh WEE uh), an American Indian woman, helped them. Later, these maps helped people travel to new land.

A **pioneer** is a person who is the first to settle in a new place. Some pioneers moved to the West because they wanted a chance to own land, build homes, and start farms or businesses. Many families used covered wagons to travel on difficult trails that crossed through rivers and mountains.

UNLOCK THE BIG ?

I will know where immigrants came from and why they settled here.

Vocabulary

immigrant

pioneer

Write how a compass and map could help explorers.

The map below shows some trails that explorers and pioneers used as they traveled to the West.

1. **Circle** places on the trails where it might have been difficult for pioneers to travel.

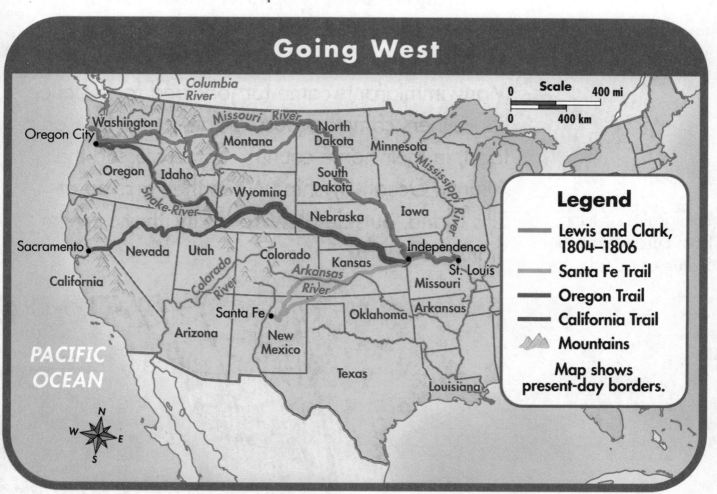

Going West

Columbia River

Scale
0 — 400 mi
0 — 400 km

Washington

Oregon City

Missouri River

Montana

North Dakota

Minnesota

Oregon

Idaho

South Dakota

Mississippi River

Snake River

Wyoming

Nebraska

Iowa

Sacramento

Nevada

Utah

Colorado

Colorado River

Arkansas River

Kansas

Independence

St. Louis

Missouri

California

Santa Fe

Arizona

New Mexico

Oklahoma

Arkansas

Texas

Louisiana

PACIFIC OCEAN

N W E S

Legend

— Lewis and Clark, 1804–1806
— Santa Fe Trail
— Oregon Trail
— California Trail
▲▲ Mountains

Map shows present-day borders.

PEARSON realize Go online to access your interactive digital lesson.

197

Not All Free

Many immigrants came to the United States for freedom. But African Americans were not free. They were brought here as slaves to work without pay. Harriet Tubman was one slave who escaped. Later, she came back to help others. She led about 300 people to freedom.

Many people thought slavery was wrong. Abraham Lincoln was one of them. He was the sixteenth President of the United States, and he worked hard to end slavery.

2. 🎯 **Fact and Opinion Underline** Abraham Lincoln's opinion about slavery.

A Nation of Immigrants

Many immigrants came for jobs and for a better life. Others came because of famine, or lack of food, in their home country. Some crossed the Atlantic Ocean by ship. When they arrived at Ellis Island, outside New York City, they saw the Statue of Liberty.

Immigrants arriving from Europe saw the Statue of Liberty.

The Statue of Liberty is a monument. It has become a symbol of freedom for all Americans. Many immigrants still come to the United States in search of freedom.

3. **Underline** a reason that immigrants move to the United States today.

TEKS 1.B, 15.A, 15.B

4. ⊙ **Cause and Effect** **Write** an effect of immigration.

_____

_____

_____

5. **?** **List** two ways the United States has changed over time.

 my Story Ideas

_____

_____

_____

_____

6. **Write** a word to complete the sentence.

The Statue of Liberty is an important monument because it is

_____

a symbol of _____ .

Technology Then and Now

Look at the photograph of a family traveling long ago.

TEKS
4.B, 4.C, 17.A, 17.B

Changes in technology over time make it easier for people to live and work.

Home Life Then and Now

People have always needed food, water, and clothing. In ancient times, people gathered plants and berries to eat. **Ancient** means a very long time ago. Later, American Indians and colonists began to use horses and simple plows to plant seeds for food. People used wooden buckets to carry water from wells. They sewed their clothes by hand.

Today, farmers use tractors to plow fields quickly. Pipes bring fresh water into our homes. Sewing machines help us to make clothes faster. Modern technology makes life easier.

1. Underline two tools from long ago.

Colonists sewed clothes by hand.

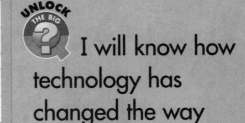

UNLOCK THE BIG ? I will know how technology has changed the way people live.

Vocabulary

ancient   telegraph

invention

Write about how you traveled to school today.

Transportation Then and Now

Long ago, horses were the fastest way to travel. There were no cars, trains, or planes. People wanted to travel more quickly. Some people came up with new ideas called inventions. An **invention** is something that is made for the first time. Karl Benz invented the car. Then Henry Ford invented a way to make a lot of cars quickly. George Stephenson invented the train. And brothers Orville and Wilbur Wright invented the airplane.

A Wright brother flying over the beach at Kitty Hawk, North Carolina

2. ◉ **Draw Conclusions Write** one way transportation inventions can be helpful.

_____

_____

_____

PEARSON realize Go online to access your interactive digital lesson.

201

Alexander Graham Bell made the first telephone call from New York to Chicago in 1892.

Thomas Edison made changes to the light bulb that helped it burn longer.

Communication Then and Now

In the past, it took a long time to communicate with others. It could take ten days to get a letter. Pony Express riders carried messages from Missouri to California by horse! Later, other inventions were used to send messages. Samuel Morse improved the **telegraph,** a way of sending coded messages over wires. In 1876, Alexander Graham Bell invented the telephone. For a long time, phones were connected by wires. Phones do not need wires to work today.

More Technology

If you had been born in 1850, your home would not have had electricity. The light in your home would have come from oil lamps and candles. Thomas Edison invented a new kind of light bulb in 1880. Many people had electricity in their homes soon after that. Today, televisions, refrigerators, and computers all need electricity to work.

Thomas Edison also invented the record player. CDs, or compact discs, were made later. Today, people can play music on their computers and cell phones.

3. **Underline** inventions you use today.

Science Helps Meet Needs

Scientists develop and test ideas that are used to create the technology we use every day. Science has even changed the way people meet their basic needs.

We can grow more food because of science. We now know how to keep away insects that eat our crops. We can also keep food fresh for a longer time by freezing and canning it. Our clothes help protect us because of new light and strong materials. Some cloth is waterproof or fireproof. Science has even made laundry soap better. Now our clothes are cleaner. Our homes have changed as well. We have new materials that make houses safer from extreme weather and fire. Our homes use less energy, too. This is because of new kinds of lights and ways to heat and cool.

Science has made us healthier, too. We now have medicines that protect us from disease and heal us when we are sick. Doctors have new tools. They can use lasers during surgery and X-rays to see broken bones. Science has also taught us more about our bodies.

4. **Circle** ways science has changed how people meet their basic needs.

Science Meets Other Needs

You can also see science at work in how we play, travel, and communicate. Science has made better sports equipment. Bicycles are lighter and go faster. Bats hit balls better. New kinds of shoes help us run faster. Science has also changed how we watch TV and read books. Televisions are now thin and flat. Hundreds of books can be stored in a small tablet.

Some trains now travel on a cushion of air created by magnets. There are no steel rails or wheels. There is not even an engine. Some new cars no longer use gas. They run on electricity. Cars may soon be able to drive themselves. Communication has changed, too. We can see and talk to people on our phones and computers. Science and technology will continue to change. We can only guess how they will change our lives in the future.

5. Write how science has changed recreation.

Modern bicycles are made to go faster.

Children can read books on a tablet.

6. **Identify** one invention that you use, and **describe** how it helps meet your needs.

Got it?

TEKS 4.B, 17.A, 17.B

7. ◉ **Fact and Opinion** Is this sentence a fact or an opinion? *The telephone is the best invention.* Which word is a clue?

---

8. ⑦ **Write** one way that technology and science have changed communication over time.

my Story Ideas

---

9. **Write** the names of two people who changed transportation and one way science is changing transportation.

Fact and Opinion

A fact is something that you can prove is true. An opinion is what someone thinks or believes. Sentences can be categorized, or grouped, as statements of fact or opinion.

Read the paragraph about Paul Revere.

Paul Revere

Many people believe that Paul Revere was the most important hero of the American Revolution. On the night of April 18, 1775, two lanterns were lit in the tower of North Church. It was the signal that the British were coming by sea. Paul Revere traveled from Boston to Lexington warning local communities so they could fight the British. This event influenced history.

The sentence *Many people believe that Paul Revere was the most important hero of the American Revolution* is an opinion. Words like *believe, feel,* and *think* tell you that a statement is an opinion. The other sentences in the paragraph are facts that can be proven.

TEKS

SS 4.C Explain how people have influenced local community history.

SS 13.B Identify historical figures such as Paul Revere who have exemplified good citizenship.

SS 13.C Identify other individuals who exemplify good citizenship.

SS 18.D Categorize information.

ELA 14.B Locate the facts that are clearly stated in a text.

1. **Write** a fact about how Paul Revere influenced history.

2. **Read** the paragraph about Florence Nightingale. Categorize statements as fact or opinion.

   Underline three facts. **Circle** three opinions.

Florence Nightingale

Florence Nightingale was a leader of nurses. She helped care for soldiers during a war. She bought supplies. She worked day and night. She had a kind heart. After the war, she started the first school for nurses. Other nurses thought she was the best teacher. She wrote the first textbook for nurses. Her work and good citizenship will never be forgotten.

American Heroes

Envision It!

Look at the photographs.

TEKS
1.B, 4.A, 4.B, 13.B, 13.C

A hero is a person who makes a difference in the lives of others.

Many Kinds of Heroes

These American heroes made our country a better place for everyone to live.

John Adams

Adams was a Founding Father and our country's second president. He helped American colonists win independence.

Benjamin Franklin

Franklin was a Founding Father and a great inventor. He started the first public library in the United States.

Dolley Madison

Madison was the wife of our fourth president, James Madison. She helped make the White House a symbol of America.

Vocabulary

civil rights
innovator

Write how these people help others.

Heroes Make a Difference

Some heroes speak out for our country and its freedom. Other heroes speak out for the rights of people. These rights are called our **civil rights.**

Sojourner Truth

W.E.B. Du Bois

George Washington Carver

Sojourner Truth (SOH jur nur TROOTH) gave many speeches around the country for the rights of African Americans and women.

W.E.B. Du Bois (doo BOYZ) was a writer and activist for African American civil rights and a founder of the NAACP.

George Washington Carver was a scientist and inventor who helped southern farmers by teaching them to rotate crops to enrich the soil.

Some heroes have new ideas that help improve our lives. We call them **innovators.** Other heroes show individualism. They take brave steps to change the way we think about our world.

Robert Fulton

Fulton built a steamboat with an engine. This steamboat could move people and goods faster than older boats.

Sequoyah

Sequoyah (si KWOI uh) invented an alphabet for the Cherokee language. It helped Cherokee people learn to read and write.

Irma Rangel

Irma Rangel was the first Hispanic woman in the Texas Legislature. She supported policies to help women, children, and minorities.

Amelia Earhart

Earhart was the first woman to fly alone across the Atlantic Ocean. She believed in women's rights.

Thurgood Marshall

Marshall was the first African American Supreme Court judge. He also worked for civil rights.

WASPs

The Women Airforce Service Pilots flew military airplanes in World War II. They were based in Houston, Texas.

1. ◉ **Main Idea and Details** Write about how Sojourner Truth helped others.

_____

- - - - - - - - - - - - - - - - - -

_____

TEKS 4.A, 4.B, 13.B, 13.C

Got it?

2. ◉ **Fact and Opinion** Write your opinion of one of the American heroes you read about.

- - - - - - - - - - - - - - - - - -

_____

3. **Think** about what life long ago was like for W.E.B. Du Bois, Irma Rangel, and other people you read about. **Write** one way that life now is different from life long ago.

my **Story Ideas**

_____

- - - - - - - - - - - - - - - - - -

_____

- - - - - - - - - - - - - - - - - -

_____

4. On a separate sheet of paper, **identify** three heroes from this lesson who showed individualism. **Write** a sentence describing a contribution that each of them made.

Lesson 1 TEKS 2.A, 2.B, 7.D

1. Write one reason that communities change over time.

Lesson 2 TEKS 3.A

2. Circle the primary sources that come from the early history of the United States.

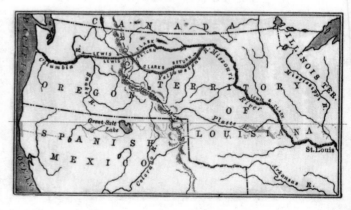

Lesson 3 TEKS 7.C

3. Fill in the blank.

American Indians used _____

_____ for their food, clothing, and shelter.

Lesson 4 TEKS 4.C, 13.B, 13.C

4. Write how John and Abigail Adams influenced their

local community.

_____

_____

_____

Lesson 5 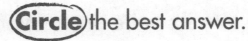 TEKS 4.C

5. Complete the sentence. (Circle) the best answer.

Immigrants are people who

A   are the first to settle and build homes in a new place.

B   are ruled by another country.

C   move from one country to another to make a new life.

Lesson 6   TEKS 17.A, 17.B

6. Write how each invention changed people's lives.

telephone: _____

airplane: _____

Lesson 7   TEKS 4.A, 4.B, 13.B

7. ◉**Fact and Opinion Read** each statement.
Write *O* for Opinion, and *F* for Fact.

___ Amelia Earhart flew alone across the Atlantic.

___ Sojourner Truth worked the hardest for civil rights.

___ The WASPs were brave World War II pilots.

___ Robert Fulton built a steamboat with an engine.

8. Fill in the blank.

Thurgood Marshall influenced the nation as a

_____

Go online to write and illustrate your own **myStory Book** using the **myStory Ideas** from this chapter.

 ## How does life change throughout history?

TEKS

SS 1.A, 19.B
ELA 17

In this chapter you have learned about history and the stories of people, places, and events of past times. You learned about how some people were not free and how others had to fight for freedom.

Think about the freedoms you enjoy every day. **Draw** a picture showing what freedom means to you. **Write** a caption for your picture.

PEARSON
realize   Go online to access your
interactive digital lesson.   215

Atlas

The United States of America, Political

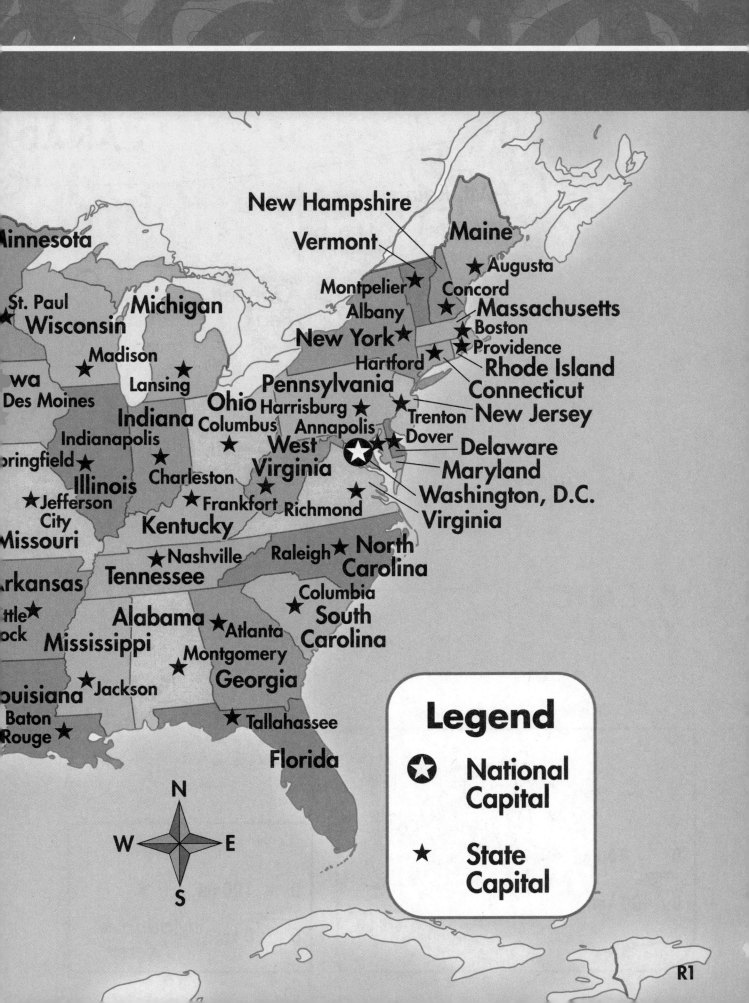

The United States of America, Physical

CANADA

▲Mt. Rainier

Rocky Mountains

Gannett Peak ▲

Great Plains

▲Mt. Elbert

Mt. Whitney ▲

PACIFIC OCEAN

Rio Grande

MEXICO

0   400 mi

0   400 km

Mt. McKinley ▲

0   100 mi

0   100 km

Mauna Kea ▲

R2

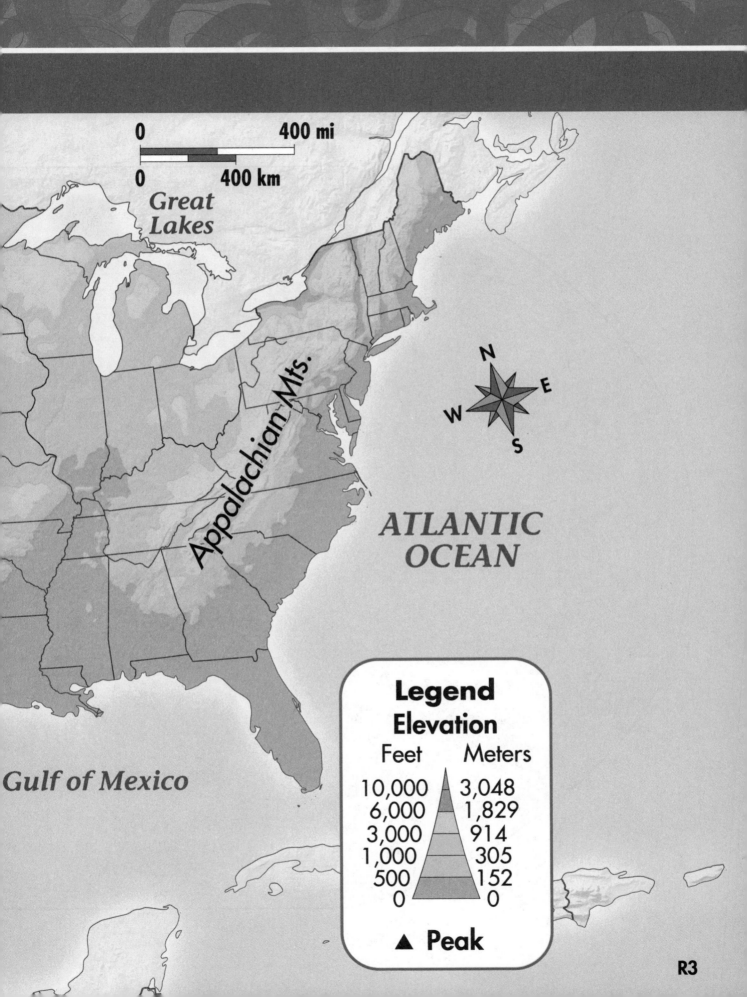

Great
Lakes

Appalachian Mts.

ATLANTIC
OCEAN

Gulf of Mexico

N

W   E

S

0   400 mi
0   400 km

Legend
Elevation

Feet	Meters
10,000	3,048
6,000	1,829
3,000	914
1,000	305
500	152
0	0

▲ Peak

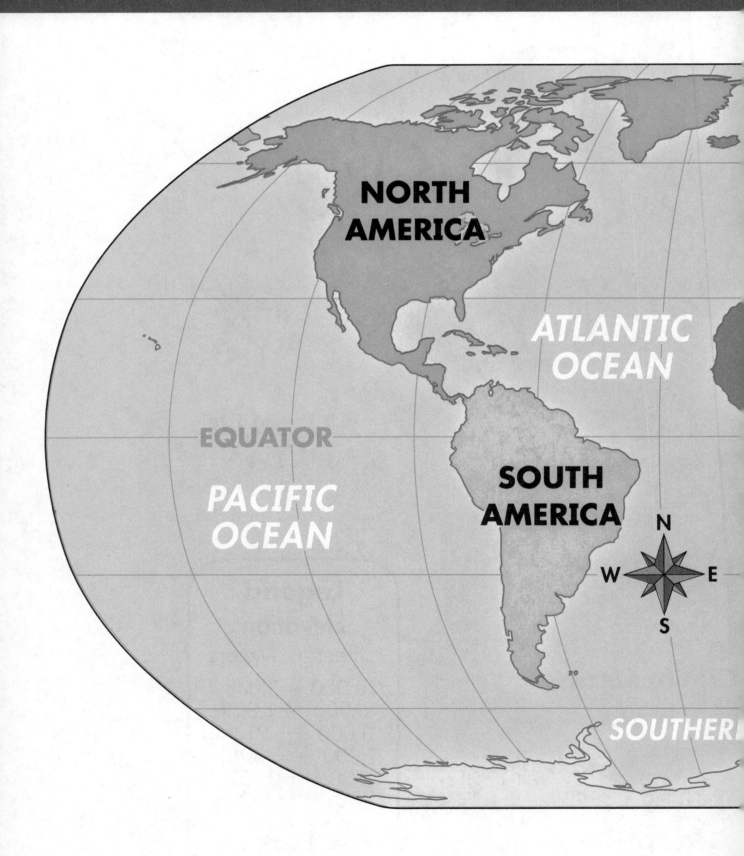

NORTH
AMERICA

ATLANTIC
OCEAN

EQUATOR

PACIFIC
OCEAN

SOUTH
AMERICA

N

W   E

S

SOUTHER

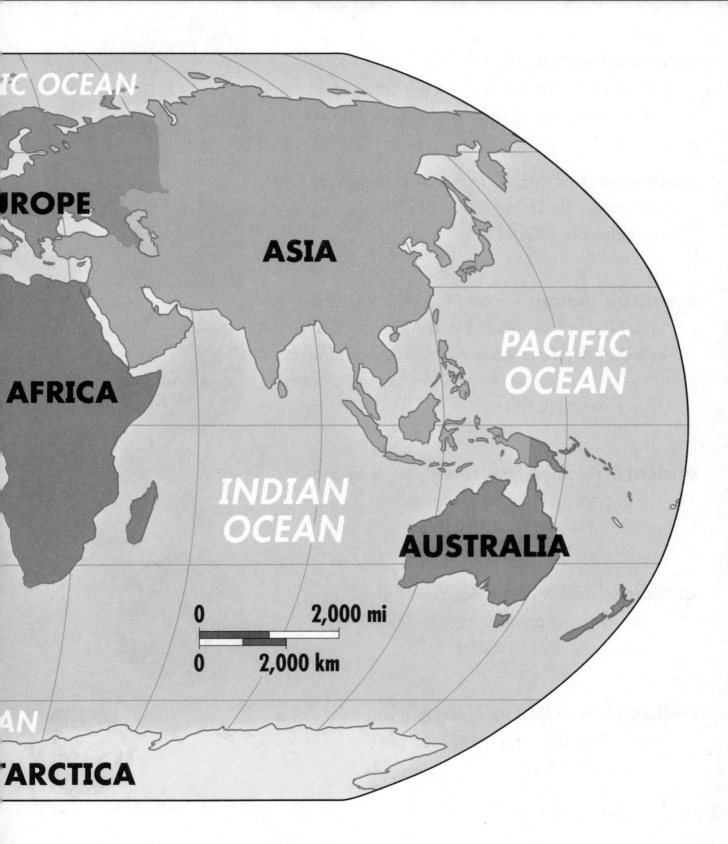

IC OCEAN

EUROPE

ASIA

PACIFIC
OCEAN

AFRICA

INDIAN
OCEAN

AUSTRALIA

0   2,000 mi

0   2,000 km

AN

ARCTICA

Glossary

A

absolute location (AB suh loot loh KAY shun) The exact spot where a place is located. Your home address is an **absolute location**. NOUN

amendment (uh MEND muhnt) A change to a document. The United States Constitution has 27 amendments. NOUN

American Indians (uh MAIR ih kun ihn DEE uhnz) The first people to live in America, also called Native Americans. Many **American Indians** were forced to leave their land when the pioneers moved west. NOUN

ancient (AYN shunt) From a very long time ago. The **ancient** wooden toys were carved by people who lived long ago. ADJECTIVE

anthem (an THUM) A patriotic song. The United States national **anthem** is called "The Star Spangled Banner." NOUN

artifact (AHR tih fakt) An object that was made long ago. This **artifact** is a good example of Pueblo pottery. NOUN

B

barter (BAHRT ur) To trade goods or services without using money. People can **barter** to get things they need. VERB

benefit (BEN uh fiht) A good result from a choice you make. One **benefit** of eating healthful foods is a healthy body. NOUN

biography (bye AH gruh fee) A book about a person's life. Jill read a **biography** about Thomas Jefferson. NOUN

borrow (BAHR oh) To use something now and pay it back later. If Tom does not have enough money, he can **borrow** some. VERB

C

cardinal direction (KAHR dnuhl duh REK shun) One of the four main directions on Earth. North is one of the four **cardinal directions**. NOUN

century (SENCH ur ee) One hundred years. About a **century** ago, people started to use cars instead of horses for transportation. NOUN

citizen (SIHT uh zuhn) A member of a community, state, and country. I am a **citizen** of the United States. NOUN

civil rights (SIHV uhl ryts) The rights of people. Cesar Chavez was a **civil rights** hero. NOUN

climate (KLYE muht) The weather a place has over a long time. Florida has a hot, wet **climate**. NOUN

coast (kohst) The place where land meets the sea or ocean. I live in Texas near the Gulf **Coast**, only a few miles from the beach. NOUN

colony (KAHL uh nee) A place that is ruled by a country far away. Each **colony** in America was ruled by England before the colonies won their independence. NOUN

communication (kuh myoo nuh KAY shun) The way people share ideas, thoughts, and information with each other. Telephones are used for **communication**. NOUN

community (kuh MYOO nuh tee) A place where people work, live, and play together. We live in a **community**. NOUN

Congress (KAHNG gruhs) The part of government that writes and votes on laws. Congress passed a law. NOUN

consequence (KAHN suh kwents) Something that happens as a result of an action. When Kayla did not do her home work, the **consequence** was that she missed recess. NOUN

conserve (kuhn SURV) To protect the resources that we use. We need to **conserve** resources for our future. VERB

consumer (kuhn SOO muhr) A person who buys and uses goods. A **consumer** can buy goods at a store. NOUN

continent (KAHN tuh nent) One of the seven largest areas of land on Earth. Asia is one of Earth's **continents**. NOUN

cost (kawst) The price of something. The **cost** of the toy is five dollars. NOUN

council (KOUN suhl) A group of people chosen by citizens to make decisions or give advice to a community leader. The city **council** decided to build a new school. NOUN

court (kort) A part of our government where it is decided if someone has broken a law. The **court** judge decided that the woman did not break a law. NOUN

culture (KUHL chur) A way of life. It is part of our **culture** in the United States to celebrate Thanksgiving. NOUN

custom (KUHS tuhm) A special way a group does something. It is a **custom** to go to a parade on Chinese New Year. NOUN

D

demand (dih MAND) The amount of something that people want. The **demand** for new computers is high. NOUN

E

environment (ihn VYE urn ment) The air, land, water, and life in a place. A city is an urban environment. NOUN

equator (ee KWAYT ur) An imaginary line that divides Earth in half. The **equator** divides Earth into the Northern and the Southern Hemispheres. NOUN

explorer (eks SPLAWR ur) A person who is the first to travel to a new place. Lewis and Clark were **explorers**. NOUN

F

fact (fakt) A part of a story that is true. It is a **fact** that George Washington was our first president. NOUN

festival (FES tuh vuhl) A celebration. We are going to eat delicious food at the Cinco de Mayo **festival**. NOUN

fiction (FIHK shun) Make-believe parts in a story. The story of Paul Bunyan is **fiction**. NOUN

folk tale (FOHLK tayl) A story from long ago that was first told aloud. Johnny Appleseed is a famous **folk tale** that many people tell. NOUN

freedom (FREED um) A citizen's right to choose what to do and say. Citizens have the **freedom** to speak up when they have something important to say. NOUN

generation (jen uh RAY shun) An age group. Children, parents, and grandparents come from three different **generations**. NOUN

geography (jee AHG ruh fee) The study of Earth. Jim looks at maps and globes in his **geography** class. NOUN

globe (glohb) A model, or small copy, of Earth. We found the location of Texas on our classroom **globe**. NOUN

goods (goodz) Things that people make or grow. Many kinds of **goods** are sold in stores. NOUN

government (GUHV urn ment) A group of people who work together to run a city, a state, or a country. The **government** of the United States makes laws. NOUN

governor (GUHV uh nur) The leader of a state. The citizens of Texas voted for a new state **governor**. NOUN

grid map (grihd map) A map with lines that cross to make squares to tell the location of a place. The **grid map** helped us find the location of the Capitol Building. NOUN

H

heritage (HAYR ih tihj) Something that is passed down through families, including cultural traditions. Tacos are a food that is part of my family's cultural **heritage**. NOUN

hero (HEE roh) Someone who is remembered for bravery or good deeds. A firefighter who saves lives is a **hero**. NOUN

history (HIHS tuh ree) The story of the past. The **history** of a community tells how the community has changed over time. NOUN

holiday (HAHL uh day) A special day. Thanksgiving is a **holiday** when families in the United States have a big dinner. NOUN

I

immigrant (IHM ih gruhnt) A person who moves from one country to another. Ann's grandfather was an **immigrant** to the United States. NOUN

income (IHN kuhm) Money that people earn. Producers sell goods to earn an **income**. NOUN

independence (ihn duh PEN duhnts) Freedom from being ruled by someone else. America won its independence from England. NOUN

innovator (IHN uh vay tur) A person who has a new idea that helps to improve our lives. Robert Fulton was an innovator who built a steamboat. NOUN

intermediate direction (ihn tur MEED ee uht duh REK shun) One of the four directions in between the cardinal directions. Northwest is one of the four intermediate directions. NOUN

invention (ihn VEN shun) Something that is made for the first time. The computer is an invention that changed the way we live. NOUN

J

journal (JUHRN uhl) A daily record of thoughts and events in a person's life. Lewis and Clark wrote a journal while they explored the West. NOUN

L

landform (LAND form) The shape of Earth's land. A mountain is a large **landform**. NOUN

landmark (LAND mahrk) A structure that is important to a particular place. The Great Wall is a famous **landmark** in China. NOUN

language (LAN gwihj) Spoken words used to communicate ideas and feelings. Many people in the United States speak the English **language**. NOUN

law (law) A rule that everyone must follow. It is a law in many states that people wear seat belts while riding in a car. NOUN

loan (lohn) Money that someone borrows. He will need a **loan** to buy a home. NOUN

M

map (map) A flat picture showing information about an area, such as the roads, water, cities, and countries. Let's check the **map** for the best route to take to San Antonio. NOUN

mayor (MAY uhr) The government leader in a town or city. The **mayor** spoke at the town meeting. NOUN

monument (MAHN yuh muhnt) A statue that honors a person, event, or idea. The Statue of Liberty is a **monument** that honors American freedom. NOUN

motto (MAHT oh) A saying that stands for an important idea. There is a **motto** on the Great Seal of the United States. NOUN

N

natural hazards (NATCH uh ruhl   HAH zurdz) A natural event that can cause damage to people, property, or the environment. Earthquakes, hurricanes, and tornadoes are **natural hazards**. NOUN

natural resource (NATCH uh ruhl   REE sors) Something in nature that is ready for us to use. Trees are a **natural resource**. NOUN

needs (needz) Things we must have to live. Food, water, and air are **needs**. NOUN

nonrenewable (nahn ree NOO uh buhl) Cannot be replaced. Coal is a **nonrenewable** resource. ADJECTIVE

O

ocean (OH shun) One of the four largest bodies of water on Earth. The Atlantic **Ocean** is east of the United States. NOUN

P

patriotic (pay tree AH tick) Showing love and support for your community, state, or country. The Texas state flag is a **patriotic** symbol. ADJECTIVE

physical map (FIHZ ih kuhl map) A map that shows Earth's land and water. Anya found the Rocky Mountains on a **physical map** of the United States. NOUN

Pilgrim (PIHL gruhm) The people who settled an English colony called Plymouth. The **Pilgrims** were not prepared for the cold New England weather. NOUN

pioneer (PYE uh neer) A person who settles in a new place first. When the eastern part of the United States got crowded, **pioneers** began to settle the West. NOUN

political map (puh LIHT ih kuhl map) A map that shows the location of places with imaginary lines called boundary lines. A political map of the United States shows the borders between the states. NOUN

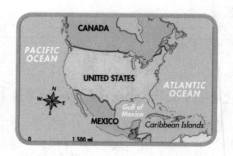

primary source (PRYE mer ee sors) Material that was written or made by someone who saw an event happen. A photograph of an event is a primary source. NOUN

prime meridian (prym muh RIHD ee uhn) An imaginary line that divides Earth in half. The prime meridian divides Earth into the Eastern and Western Hemispheres. NOUN

producer (proh DOO sur) A person who makes or grows a good. A farmer is a producer. NOUN

region (REE juhn) An area that shares special features. The Great Plains region of the United States has flat land. NOUN

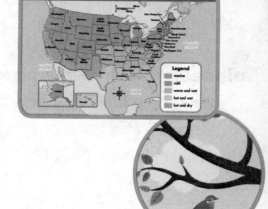

relative location (REL uh tihv loh KAY shun) The place where something is when compared to another thing. *Above* is a word that tells a relative location. NOUN

renewable (ree NOO uh buhl) Can be replaced. Wind is a **renewable** resource. ADJECTIVE

resource (REE sors) Something that is useful. Water is a **resource**. NOUN

respect (ree SPEKT) Concern for others. Good citizens show **respect** for each other. NOUN

responsible (ree SPAHN suh buhl) To take care of important things. **Responsible** citizens help clean up their communities. ADJECTIVE

right (ryt) Something that people are free to do. Citizens have the **right** to vote. NOUN

ruins (ROO uhnz) Buildings that were lived in long ago. Many people visit the Aztec **ruins** in Mexico. NOUN

rural (RUHR uhl) Having small towns and farms. Carolyn lives on a farm in a **rural** area. ADJECTIVE

S

save (sayv) To keep your money to use later. Kate will **save** her money to buy a bike. VERB

savings (SAYV ihngz) Income that you do not spend right away. In four weeks, Yoshi will use his **savings** to buy a game. NOUN

scarce (skairs) Not enough of something. We have to make choices when resources are **scarce**. ADJECTIVE

secondary source (SEK uhn dair ee sors) Material that was written or made by someone who did not see an event happen. An encyclopedia is a **secondary source**. NOUN

service (SUHR vihs) A job a person does for you. A barber provides a **service** when he cuts your hair. NOUN

settle (SET uhl) To live in a place or area. People choose to **settle** in different places. VERB

settler (SET luhr) A person who makes a home in a new land. European **settlers** started Plymouth Plantation. NOUN

skill (skihl) The ability to do something well. Learning how to read is an important **skill**. NOUN

specialize (SPESH uh lyz) To do one kind of thing very well. Some teachers **specialize** in teaching music. VERB

suburban (SUH bur buhn) Close to a city where people live. Port Washington is a **suburban** community near New York City. ADJECTIVE

supply (suh PLYE) How much there is of something. Boston has a large **supply** of fish. NOUN

Supreme Court (suh PREEM kort) The highest court in our country. The **Supreme Court** decided the law was not fair. NOUN

symbol (SIHM buhl) 1. An object that stands for something else. The bald eagle is a **symbol** of the United States. NOUN 2. A picture that stands for something real. She found the **symbol** for a mountain on the map. NOUN

T

tall tale (tawl tayl) A story that starts off sounding true, but is mostly fiction. The story of John Henry is a famous **tall tale**. NOUN

tax (taks) Money that is collected by the government from the citizens. **Taxes** are used to pay for schools. NOUN

technology (tek NAHL oh jee) The use of skills and tools. We use **technology** to make our work easier. NOUN

telegraph (TE leh graf) A way of sending messages over wires. The **telegraph** made it easier for people to communicate. NOUN

temperature (TEHM pur uh tyur) How hot or cold something is. The **temperature** outside is 64 degrees. NOUN

trade (trayd) To buy, sell, or exchange goods or services with someone else. People can use money to **trade** for things they need. VERB

tradition (truh DIHSH uhn) Something that is passed down over time. It is a **tradition** in Brian's family to have a big dinner each Sunday. NOUN

transportation (trans por TAY shun) A way to move people and things from place to place. A car is one kind of **transportation**. NOUN

U

urban (ur BUHN) Made up of a city and the places around it. Jean lives in an **urban** area. ADJECTIVE

V

veteran (VET uh ruhn) Someone who has served in the armed forces. Mr. Lee is a **veteran** of World War II. NOUN

vote (voht) To make a choice that can be counted. Citizens in the United States **vote** for the president. VERB

W

wants (wahnts) Things that we would like to have, but do not need to live. A toy and a bike are **wants**. NOUN

weather (WETH ur) What it is like outside at a certain time and place. Today's **weather** is sunny and warm. NOUN

Index

This index lists the pages on which topics appear in this book. Page numbers followed by *m* refer to maps. Page numbers followed by *p* refer to photographs. Page numbers followed by *c* refer to charts or graphs. Page numbers followed by *t* refer to timelines. Bold page numbers indicate vocabulary definitions. The terms *See* and *See also* direct the reader to alternate entries.

D

Dams, 120
Decision making, 60–63. *See also*
    Choices
    benefits in, 61–62
    by consumers, 65
    costs in, 61–62
    by producers, 65
Declaration of Independence, 156,
    194, 194*p*
Demand, 77
Diary, as primary source, 182
Directions
    cardinal, 98
    intermediate, 99
    on maps and globes, 96,
      98–99
Doctors, 71
Drilling, for oil, 118
Drivers, laws for, 30
Dry weather, 112
Du Bois, W.E.B., 209, 209*p*

E

Earhart, Amelia, 210, 210*p*
Earning money, 56, 64
Earth
    globe as model of, 103
    making changes to, 134
    resources of, 128–131
    shape of, 102
    world map of, 106
Earthquakes, 123
Eastern Hemisphere, 106
Economics
    bartering, 76
    benefits, 61–62
    borrowing money, 82–83
    buying, 53
    choices, 57, 60
    consumers, 53, 61–62, 64
    costs, 61–62
    decision making, 61–63, 65
    getting loans, 82–83
    goods, 64, 76
    income, 64
    money as a resource, 56
    needs, 52, 56, 87
    producers, 53, 64, 65, 77
    resources, 56

    savings, 80, 81
    scarcity, 58
    supply and demand, 77
    taxes, 34, 72
    trade, 76, 78, 79
Ecuador, trade with, 79
Edison, Thomas, 202, 202*p*
Education, of self, 25
Effect, 126
Electric cars, 204
Electronic sources, 185
***Elissa,* USS (ship),** 37, 37*p*
Ellis Island, 198
Encyclopedias
    as reference materials, 184
    as secondary source, 183*p*
    using parts of, 186
Energy, 128, 129, 129*c*, 203
England, American Revolution and,
    194
English settlers, 192–195
Enterprise, Alabama, 178–179
Environment, 116
    changing by taking resources,
      118–119
    changing to make life easier,
      120–121
    rural, **117**
    suburban, **117**
    urban, **116–117**
Envision It!, 16, 22, 28, 34, 40, 44,
    56, 60, 64, 70, 76, 80, 92, 96,
    102, 108, 112, 116, 128, 132,
    144, 148, 154, 158, 162, 176,
    182, 188, 192, 196, 200, 208
Equality, and good citizens, 23
Equator, 103
Ethnic celebrations, 148–150
Europe, 102
Explorer, 192
Express ideas
    orally, 2
    written material, 3
Extreme weather, 123

F

Fact, 158, 206
Families
    choices made by, 58, 60
    history of, 176
    as primary source, 184
    then and now, 177

Farming
    American Indian, 188, 190
    boll weevil and destruction of
      cotton, 178
    Carver, George Washington, 209
    crops, 178–179
    irrigation of land for, 121
    modifying land for, 121
    in rural communities, 124
    technology and, 200
Federal government, 36
Festival, 148
"Festival Time," 141
Fiction, 158
Firefighters, 72
Fire protection, as government
    service, 72
Fishing, 122
Flags
    American, 44, 45, 45*p*, 159
    Chinese, 164
    Mexican, 163
    Texas, 6
Floods, 115
Flowcharts, 68–69
Flowers
    national, 46, 46*p*
    state, 6, 6*p*
Folk tales, 158–159. *See also* Tall
    tales
    Crockett, Davy, 158
    Johnny Appleseed, 159
    Ross, Betsy, 159
Food, 144
    delivering supplies in
      emergencies, 135
    science to help grow, 203
    soil for growing, 122
Forests, as natural resource, 122
Founders, 178
Founding Fathers
    Adams, John, 208
    Franklin, Benjamin, 208
France, 149
    Statue of Liberty as gift from, 38
Franklin, Benjamin, 208, 208*p*
Freedom, 24
    monuments honoring, 38
    protection of, by Bill of Rights,
      1, 24
Freedom of speech, 1
Free enterprise system, 57
Fresh water, 109
Fulton, Robert, 210, 210*p*
Future, 176

K

Keywords, for Internet search, 185
King, Martin Luther, Jr., 156–157, 157p

L

Lake, 109
Land
  effect of people on, 116–118
  irrigation of, 121
Land clearing, for urban development, 117
Landforms, 108
  hills, 108, 134
  islands, 109
  on maps and globes, 110
  mountains, 108, 134
  peninsula, 109
  on physical maps, 110
  plains, 108
  plateaus, 108
  valleys, 108
Landmarks, 8–9, 37, **165**
  significance of in community, 8
  significance of in nation, 37
  significance of in state, 8, 9, 37
  Texas State Capitol, 9
  United States Capitol, 37
  USS *Elissa,* 37
  White House, 37
Language, 144
  Navajo, 146–147
Lasers, 203
Latitude, 106
Laws, 29
  community, 29–31, 40
  consequences for breaking, 31
  importance of, 30
  state, 35, 41
Leaders
  community, 40, 72, 156–157
  government, 72, 156
  of state government, 41
  of United States government, 36, 42–43, 72
Legend
  on globe, 11
  on map, 10, 97, 101, 105
Lewis, Meriwether, 196
Liberty Bell, 47, 47p
Librarians, 70, 72

Libraries
  first, in United States, 208
  as government service, 34
  reference materials in, 184
  Web sites, 185
Life
  changes in, throughout history, 215
  choosing where to live, 122–125
  making easier, 120–121
Light bulbs, 202
Lincoln, Abraham, 198
Literature, as source, 183. *See also* Folk tales; Stories; Tall tales
"Living in America," 173
Loan, 82
  getting, from bank, 82–83
Local history, 184
Locating
  communities on maps and globes, 10, 11
  major cities in Texas, 100
  the state capital on maps and globes, 10, 42m, 105
Location
  absolute, 93
  relative, 92
  use of globes to show, 104, 105
  use of maps to show, 94
Longitude, 106

M

Madison, Dolley, 208, 208p
Magazines, as reference materials, 184
Magnetic trains, 204
Main idea, identifying, 74
Mankiller, Wilma, 191, 191p
Map
  create a, 95–97, 101
  defined, 96
  Going West, 197m
  grid, 94
  interpreting, 10
  legend, 97, 101, 105
  locations on, 94
  orientation, 98–99, 103, 104, 106
  Our Town, 98m
  parts of, 97
  physical, 110
  political, 100m, 111
  reasons for using, 96

  as reference materials, 184
  road, 133
  Rock Trail, 97m
  scale, 100–101
  The Southeast, Natural Resources, 130m
  symbols on, 97, 110
  Texas, Political, 10m, 100m
  Texas Road Map, 133m
  Three American Indian Groups, 189m
  United States Capitals, 42m
  United States Climate Regions, 114m
  The United States, Physical, 110m
  United States Trade, 78m
  Washington, D.C., 94, 94m
  western settlement, 197
  world, 106
  The World, 107m
Map routes
  of community, 101
  of home, 95, 97
  of school, 95, 96
Map scale, 100–101
Map Skills
  legend, 101
  map scale, 100–101
Mardi Gras, 149, 149p
Mariachi bands, 148
Marshall, Thurgood, 210, 210p
Mayor, 40, 72
Medicine, delivering emergency supplies of, 135
Memorial Day, 155
Mexico
  on maps and globes, 105
  symbol of, 163
Mexico City, culture in, 162–163
Mockingbird, 6, 6p
Money
  borrowing, 82–83
  earning, 56, 64
  as a resource, 56
  saving, 80–82
  spending, 80, 81
Monuments, 8–9, 38, **179**
  significance of, 8
Morse, Samuel, 202
Moss, 113
Motto, 46
Mountains, 108, 108m, 134
Museums, 124
  learning about history in, 184
  Web sites, 185

Credits

Text Acknowledgments

Grateful acknowledgement is made to the following for copyrighted material:

Page 3
Texas Tech University
"Anthem" from Buck Ramsey's Grass: With Essays on His Life and Work. Copyright (c) 2005 by Texas Tech University Press. Used by permission.

Note: Every effort has been made to locate the copyright owner of material reproduced in this component. Omissions brought to our attention will be corrected in subsequent editions.

Maps

XNR Productions, Inc.

Photographs

Photo locators denoted as follows: Top (T), Center (C), Bottom (B), Left (L), Right (R), Background (Bkgd)

Cover

Front Cover (TL) Sam Houston statue, TobicPhoto/Fotolia; (TR) Palo Duro Canyon State Park, mikenorton/Shutterstock; (CC) Bluebonnet, Randy Heisch/Shutterstock; (CR) McDonald Observatory, Chris Howes/Wild Places Photography Photography/Alamy; (BC) Kemah Boardwalk, Galveston Bay, George Doyle/Stockbyte/Getty Images.
Back Cover (TR) Houston skyline, Jörg Hackemann/Fotolia; (CL) Police officers, Jacky Chapman/Alamy; (CR) Texas cattle ranch, Tom Payne/Alamy; (BC) Boy scouts at Walker Creek Elementary School, North Richland Hills, J Burleson/Alamy.

Text

Front Matter
x: Pearson Education; xi: discpicture/Alamy; xii: NASA/Corbis; xiii: Steve Skjold/Alamy; xiv: Vintage Images/Alamy Images

Celebrate Texas and the Nation
001: INSADCO Photography/Alamy; 001: Lilya Espinosa/Shutterstock; 002: okalinichenko/Fotolia; 002: Yellow Dog Productions/Digital Vision/Getty Images; 004: University of Texas at San Antonio Libraries Special Collections; 005: Architect of the Capitol; 006: John Zellmer/E+/Getty Images; 006: Micah Young/E+/Getty Images; 006: Steve Byland/Fotolia; 007: Gabe Palmer/Alamy; 007: Sherry Moore/Alamy; 008: © 2012 John Rogers; 008: Sally Scott/Shutterstock; 008: State Preservation Board, Austin, Texas; 009: Brandon Seidel/Shutterstock; 009: Kevin Dietsch/UPI/Newscom; Andersen Ross/Blend Images/Corbis

Chapter 01
012: Pearson Education; 016: Purestock/Getty Images; 017: Pearson Education; 018: AP images; 018: Tom Grill/Corbis; 022: Pearson Education; 022: Steve Helber/AP Images; 023: Sean Justice/Corbis; 023: Susan Biddle/The Washington Post/Getty Images; 025: Dmitriy Shironosov/Shutterstock; 026: Leland Bobbé/Corbis; 028: Lev Kropotov/Shutterstock; 028: Stephen Bonk/Shutterstock; 029: White/PhotoLibrary; 031: Robert J. Beyers II/Shutterstock; 036: Wally McNamee/CORBIS; 038: Q-Images/Alamy; 041: Education & Exploration 1/Alamy Stock Photo; 043: Haraz N. Ghanbari/AP Images; 044: Andersen Ross/Stockbyte/Getty Images; 045: Susan Montgomery/Shutterstock; 046: James Young/DK Images; 046: NA; 047: Racheal Grazias/Shutterstock; Brandon Seidel/Shutterstock; James Nielsen/AP Images; Larry Williams/Corbis; Library of Congress Prints and Photographs Division[LC-USZC4-594]; Michael Moran/DK Images,Ltd; Orhan Çam/Fotolia

Chapter 02
052: Pearson Education; 056: Gemenacom/Shutterstock; 056: Richard Price/Getty Images; 057: Enshpil/Shutterstock; 057: lecic/Fotolia; 057: Tatjana Brila/Shutterstock; 060: Aprilphoto/Shutterstock; 061: DK Images,; 061: Hemera Technologies/PhotoObjects/Thinkstock; 064: Witold Skrypczak/Alamy; 065: Stuart O'Sullivan/The Image Bank/Getty Images; 066: Hans L Bonnevier/Johner Images/Alamy; 067: Martin Heying/vario images GmbH & Co.KG/Alamy; 070: Hill Street Studios/Blend Images/Corbis; 070: Lisa F Young/Shutterstock; 070: Patti McConville/Alamy; 071: Wave break Media Micro/Fotolia; 072: Richard Lewisohn/Getty Images; 073: Tetra Images/Getty Images; 076: Bob Jacobson/Corbis; 076: Lisa F. Young/Fotolia; 077: Joshua Roper/Alamy; 079: John Glover/Alamy; 080: discpicture/Alamy; 085: Andersen Ross/Photolibrary; 56: Dhoxax/Shutterstock; 57: bocky/Shutterstock; 60: Elena Schweitzer/Shutterstock; aijohn784/Fotolia; Morgan Lane Photography/Shutterstock

Chapter 03
088: Pearson Education; 094: Hoberman Collection UK/Alamy; 096: Hemera/Thinkstock; 096: istockphoto/Thinkstock; 102: Comstock/Jupiterimages/Thinkstock; 102: NASA/Corbis; 103: Morgan Lane Photograph/Shutterstock; 108: Banana Stock/Photolibrary; 108: Hemera/Thinkstock; 109: Bill Stevenson/PhotoLibrary; 109: iStockphoto/Thinkstock; 112: Masterfile; 112: Paul Tomlins/Flowerphotos/PhotoLibrary; 113: Gavriel Jecan/Danita Delimont/Alamy; 113: Mark Hamblin/Oxford Scientific (OSF)/PhotoLibrary; 113: Rob Casey/Stone/Getty Images; 115: A. T. Willett/Alamy; 116: Carroteater/Shutterstock; 119: Morgan Lane Photography/Shutterstock; 120: Ken Inness/Shutterstock; 120: Patrick Eden/Alamy; 121: Tish1/Shutterstock; 122–123: Joseph Sohm/Visions of America, LLC/Alamy; 123: Mike Theiss/Ultimate Chase/Corbis News/Corbis; 124: Jose Luis Magana/AFP/Getty Images/Newscom; 124: MyShotz.com/Fotolia; 125: Craig Ruttle/Alamy; 128: Anthony Cottrell/

Shutterstock; 128: DK Images; 128: Mary Beth Bueno/Alamy; 128: Richard Drury/Getty Images; 129: Andersen Ross/Getty Images; 129: Blend Images/Alamy; 129: Gorilla/Fotolia; 130: Eye Ubiquitous/SuperStock; 130: Q-Images/Alamy; 131: Mike Flippo/Shutterstock; 132: 3d brained/Shutterstock; 132: Andersen Ross/Blend Images/Corbis; 132: Stockbyte/Thinkstock; 134: Jim Parkin/Alamy; Morgan Lane Photography/Shutterstock

Chapter 04

140: Pearson Education; 144: Kheng Guan Toh,2010/Shutterstock; 144: pilipphoto - Fotolia.com; 144: Yadid Levy/Robert Harding Picture Library/AGE Fotostock; 145: Angelo Cavalli/SuperStock; 146: DK Images; 148: jgi/Blend Images/Corbis; 148: Steve Skjold/Alamy; 150: Judy Bellah/Alamy; 152: DK Images; 152: Official U. S. Marine Corps photo; 152: Peter Cade/Iconica/Getty Images; 154: Ariel Skelley/Blend Images/Photolibrary; 155: Bill Haber/AP Images; 155: Visions of America, LLC/Alamy; 156: The Granger Collection, NYC; 157: Paul Martinka/Polaris/Newscom; 162: chiakto/Shutterstock; 162: Library of Congress Prints and Photographs Division [LC-DIG-ppmsca-35700]; 163: Dmitry Rukhlenko/Shutterstock; 163: granata1111/Shutterstock; 163: Laurie Barr/Shutterstock; 164: ekler/Shutterstock; 164: Tom Stoddart Archive/Getty Images; 165: Tomas Slavicek/Shutterstock; 166: Dmitry Rukhlenko/Shutterstock; 166: Kheng Guan Toh/Shutterstock; 166: pilipphoto - Fotolia.com; 166: Tomas Slavicek/Shutterstock; 168: chiakto/Shutterstock; 168: DK Images; 168: Judy Bellah/Alamy; 168: Steve Skjold/Alamy; 168: pilipphoto - Fotolia.com; 169: Ariel Skelley/Blend Images/PhotoLibrary; 169: Library of Congress Prints and Photographs Division[LC-USZ62-122982]; 169: Visions of America, LLC/Alamy; 170: Alan Bailey/Rubberball/Corbis; 170: Tom Stoddart Archive/Getty Images

Chapter 05

172: Pearson Education; 176: Image Source/Alamy; 176: Jo Foord/Getty Images; 176: MNStudio/Shutterstock; 177: Monkey Business Images/Shutterstock; 179: Witold Skrypczak/Alamy; 180: Austin History Center, Austin Public Library; 181: J Marshall/Tribaleye Images/Alamy; 181: Jim Bennett/Corbis; 182: North Wind Picture Archives/Alamy; 182: University of Texas at San Antonio Libraries Special Collections; 183: Brand X Pictures/Getty Images; 183: JTB Photo/SuperStock; 183: photogl/Shutterstock; 184: Comstock/Thinkstock; 185: iStockphoto/Thinkstock; 185: The Granger Collection, NYC; 186: Pearson Education; 188: Accent Alaska.com/Alamy; 188: Danita Delimont/Alamy; 188: M. Timothy O'Keefe/Alamy; 191: Jerry Willis/AP Images; 194: The Art Archive/Alamy; 196: haveseen/Shutterstock; 196: North Wind Picture Archives/Alamy; 198: Edwin Levick/Getty Images; 199: gracious_tiger/Shutterstock; 200: Peter Byron/Photo Edit; 200: Vintage Images/

Alamy; 201: Charles Phelps Cushing/ClassicStock/Alamy; 202: The Granger Collection, NYC; 203: H. Mark Weidman/Alamy; 204: Mar Photographics/Alamy; 204: Wong Sze Fei/Fotolia; 208: Hermera/Thinkstock; 208: Rick Gomez/Comet/Corbis; 209: AP Images; 209: Library of Congress Prints and Photographs Division[LC-USZ62-16767]; 210: Corbis; 210: Deborah Cannon/AP Images; 210: Lightroom Photos/Alamy; 212: Brand X Pictures/Getty Images; 212: haveseen/Shutterstock.com; 212: North Wind Picture Archives/Alamy; 212: North Wind Picture Archives/Alamy

Glossary

R06: Dorling Kindersley; R06: SuperStock; R07: Brand X Pictures/Getty Images; R07: Shalom Ormsby/Blend Images/Corbis; R07: Underwood & Underwood/Corbis; R08: Cathy Murphy/Hulton Archive/Getty Images; R08: Masterfile; R08: Steve Helber/AP Images; R08: Stockbyte/Thinkstock; R08: Wally McNamee/Corbis; R09: Bob Jacobson/Corbis; R09: Mike Flippo/Shutterstock; R09: Robert J. Beyers II/Shutterstock; R10: Alex Mares-Manton/Asia Images/Corbis; R10: JGI/Blend Images/Corbis; R10: Judy Bellah/Alamy; R10: Mark Hamblin/Oxford Scientific (OSF)/PhotoLibrary Group Inc./Getty Images; R10: Morgan Lane Photograph/Shutterstock; R10: scoutingstock/Alamy; R11: NASA; R12: Henri conodul/Photolibrary/Getty Images; R12: Martin Heying/vario images GmbH & Co.KG/Alamy; R12: Monkey Business Images, 2009/Shutterstock; R12: Pearson; R13: Ariel Skelley/Blend Images/Photolibrary/Getty Images; R13: discpicture/Alamy; R13: Edwin Levick/Getty Images; R13: Hermera/Thinkstock; R13: Kheng Guan Toh/Shutterstock; R13: Vintage Images/Alamy; R13: Witold Skrypczak/Alamy; R14: Getty Images; R14: Granger Collection; R14: North Wind Picture Archives/Alamy; R14: Racheal Grazias/Shutterstock; R14: Tomas Slavicek/Shutterstock; R15: Hemera/Thinkstock; R15: White/Photolibrary/Getty Images; R15: Yadid Levy/Robert Harding Picture Library/AGE Fotostock; R16: gracious_tiger/Shutterstock; R16: public domain; R18: Bluford W. Muir/Corbis; R18: Stuart O'Sullivan/The Image Bank/Getty Images; R19: carroteater/Shutterstock; R19: Dorling Kindersley; R19: Purestock/Getty Images; R19: Susan Biddle/The Washington Post; R19: Tom Grill/Corbis; R20: Yellow Dog Productions Inc.; R21: Dmitry Rukhlenko/Shutterstock; R21: Wave break Media Micro/Fotolia; R21: Joshua Roper/Alamy; R21: Konstantin L/Shutterstock; R21: photogl/Shutterstock; R21: Richard Lewisohn/Getty Images; R21: visuelldesign/Shutterstock; R22: 3d brained/Shutterstock; R22: Lisa F. Young/Fotolia; R22: Paul Chesley/Stone/Getty Images; R22: Rob Casey/Getty Images; R23: EuroStyle Graphics/Alamy; R23: Gemenacom/Shutterstock; R23: Ken Inness/Shutterstock; R23: Pearson Education; R23: Visions of America, LLC/Alamy